"A little Indian brave before he was ten

Played war games in the woods with his Indian friends

And he built up a dream that when he grew up

He would be a fearless warrior Indian Chief

Many moons passed and more the dream grew strong until

Tomorrow he would sing his first war song and fight his first battle

But something went wrong surprise attack killed him in his sleep that night

And so castles made of sand melts into the sea, eventually."

— ***Jimi Hendrix***

    The first time I heard this song, I was about 17 years old. Some lyrics just seem to stick with a person and these lyrics stuck with me. The title of this book actually stems from the tragedy of this young Indian brave. Just as he is closing in on his dream, it is ripped from him by a better planned and organized opponent.

    I am a product of such a "castle made of sand." The purpose of this book is to arm you, the parent, with information so that your child's dreams do not "melt into the sea." As your children walk the fairways and build the dream of becoming a college (or even a professional) golfer, it is important for you to be the educated "tribal elder."

    I wrote this book to present a process to create a disciplined, defined, and loving environment for a junior golfer. Junior golfers striving to fulfill dreams while dealing with their gamut of emotions greatly benefit from such a supportive atmosphere.

    Although PGA Professionals win awards and accolades for their ability to teach golf, they are a small part of the team. Parents are the most important part of the team because you guide your children into the mindset they will carry the rest of their lives.

Think of the pages that follow as a manual. The emphasis will, of course, be on your children. If you read deeply enough, however, I think you will find a few tips for yourself. We only have one shot. So, let's team up and help your children build "castles made of stone."

VJ Trolio

DRIVEN

Many parents are driven to remove obstacles in the way of their offspring. Sometimes obstacles are physical. Sometimes obstacles are mental. Sometimes obstacles simply stem from a lack of knowledge. Whether the situation involves poor grades, a reading comprehension problem, a lack of confidence, or even the wrong golf equipment—nearly all of us share a sense of urgency for our children.

There are two approaches, however, for how parents deal with this sense of urgency. One approach is consistent with individual's being in total control of their own destiny. The other approach is consistent with the thought that individual's are not in total control of their own destiny. The first camp suggests that we make decisions and perform actions in order to sharpen ourselves. The later camp suggests that we make decisions and perform actions to be sharpened. The first approach is "self-grooming" and the second is a "we are being groomed" approach.

Personally, I believe in the "we are being groomed" approach. One of the many ways I am being groomed has always been through the game of golf. My passion for this game has taken me many places for many different reasons. In the beginning, it was a place mostly of independence and fun. Later, the game took me to competitive places. Over the past decade, the game has primarily taken me to places of learning and teaching. What amazes me is that the game of golf is still all of these places for me.

Of all the wonders that God has created, human beings stand atop the list. As a human race, century after century, we have been driven. I need to point out something obvious: **The communities of people I find *everywhere* are still DRIVEN**. Whether it is competing, sharing knowledge, teaching, or learning, we all have an instinctual drive in common. We humans have always had this sense of drive. At one point we were hunters and gatherers, and then we became explorers looking for new lands. Even when the accepted thinking was that the world was flat, humans were driven to sail out to where the sky met the water.

In the world we live in, the seas, the moon, and even distant planets have been discovered and visited by humans or their machines. We have conquered, destroyed, saved, and given peace to countless millions. But what do we find ourselves doing in the current modern world? We are turning to ourselves and our families. We are turning inward.

Sports Psychology did not exist 100 years ago. The idea of the Self Image arose in the 1950's and was clearly covered in *Psycho-Cybernetics* during the 1970's. Freud's theory of the Id and Williams James' concept of Positive Thinking were focused on this newly discovered human drive—the drive to fix oneself. The simple reason sports psychology arose was that humans want better outcomes. You want a better body. You want to feel comfortable in a room. You want to be good public speaker. You want to finish first—on top of the heap.

Researchers have looked at the origin of sports. It seems that sports, from bowling to skeet shooting, stem from having our needs being met. Humans moved for centuries. If you wanted it, you had to go get it. We jumped, threw, and climbed. All this movement turned into sport. Over the centuries, as our race was graced with food, safety, and shelter, our drives led to the multitude of sports that we now enjoy.

In fact, humans actually pay to watch the best at the sports we love because they show us just how good a driven human can become. You can visit your local grocery store and have access to hundreds of specialized magazines with the most driven peering back at you.

The human drive works in a continuum. No matter where you find your problem, there is an answer. Not only is there an answer, there is an example of some other human that was driven to perfect that which you find wrong with yourself. Now you can pay them, or their company, to teach you how they were able to overcome the problem. Sadly, however, as we look for answers, many times the answers don't "take."

Here is a possible problem. The Driven Human is looking for ways to influence an outcome. We know who won the Masters last year. That is, the Driven Human **is not looking for the knowledge of the process**. An understanding of a process into which we plug knowledge and answers is vital to being successful.

You should know that I am also a Driven Human. My passion centers mostly on the world of golf. For the past 12 years, I have taught, or rather given, people an incentive to become better at the sport called golf. What I have learned reminds me of a simple parable from Jesus found in Luke. The parable concerns a planted tree. After three seasons, the tree did not bear fruit. The owner of the property asked his gardener to pull up the tree. The gardener requested that the owner wait one more season. In the coming spring, the gardener said he **will dig around the tree and replace some of the soil with fertilizer**. If the tree does not bear fruit, then the gardener will take it down.

I only wish this were the case for all of us Driven Humans. We often see our child not producing and we immediately want to fix this poor outcome. So what is your urgent obligation? Did it arise because you or your son or daughter did not perform well last week on the course? Did it arise because there was an episode in competition that somehow brought out a failure? Did it arise because of the performance of another athlete?

People walk into my shop all the time with problems with their golf games. They walk in with problems with their body. They walk in with problems with their brains. Trust me, these individuals are driven. The only problem is, they can't tell me their problem. Immediately the discussion (if I let them) turns to ball flight or scores. Immediately they jump to the outcome and want to know how to fix it!

Getting better at anything is a process of elimination and a process of defining how you eliminated the obstacle. But what eliminates the obstacle? Is it the mind? Is it the body? Is it the mechanics of the motion? As a general rule, I ask these questions. In a sense I am saying, "OK tree, you aren't producing any fruit. I get that. But what makes up your soil?"

It is apparent to me that individuals drive themselves in different ways. It is also clear that changing or altering that drive so that it leads to better performance is handled quite differently among individuals. This difference is why there are essentially three forms of psychology: **Cognitive, Constraint,** and **Behavioral**. While we lie awake driven to fix our children, or ourselves, we come up with plans. These plans are all laid in the foundation of one of these areas of Psychology.

Understand that we, as humans, rarely care until we are emotionally involved. Just go to a little league baseball game to understand what "being emotionally involved" looks like. For example, an eight-year old girl steps into the batter's box.

- **Story One**. She hits a scorcher at the third baseman and, to *his* father's dismay; the ball goes right between his feet. The runners on second and third score the tying and winning runs. The error by the third baseman helped decide the outcome. Now who do you think got scolded? Who do you think got the praise?

- **Story Two**. To *her* father's dismay, she looks at three straight strikes—the bat never leaving her shoulder. The pitcher's parents go bonkers. Her ineptitude strands the runners and the game is lost. Now who do you think got the praise? Who do you think got scolded?

Let's put a similar example into a golf tournament.

- **Story One**. A young man is eight over par in his first 12 holes, but then makes six straight birdies to shoot 74. Is the parent angry or frustrated?

- **Story Two**. A young man is four under par through 12 holes, but finished with six straight bogies to shoot 74. Is the parent angry or frustrated?

Driven we are. Driven to heal, steal, help, and sometimes destroy. Will our drive ever change? Has anyone changed it? Do we all think the same way? The answer to the last question is all around you. 95% of the people do the losing. 5% of the people do 95% of the winning. Essentially, 95% of us are castles made of sand. As long as the tide doesn't come in too far we will be ok. But as the wind, rain, and tide roll in farther, we falter.

Suppose, however, preparation mattered more than the performance. That is, what if we cared more about the fertilizer around the tree than how much fruit it bore? What if our castles were made of stone rather than of sand? What if the process of building the castle were laid out so well that no matter how big the wave, we could recover?

I believe such a process can be built. I believe we can turn our drive toward being helpful on the golf course and other areas of our lives. I have seen it happen and I work to make it happen with everyone that walks in the door of my shop. The reason I believe we can turn our drive toward being helpful is as follows. In 12 years, I have been a part of approximately 50 state championships. I have been a part of two individuals making it to the Semi-Finals of USGA Championships and the only First Team All-American born in Mississippi. I have been a part of success on the Nationwide and PGA Tour. These people are not built differently from other people. The difference, however, is simple: their drive is anchored in things that they can control. Those that do not bear as much fruit are generally more concerned with the fruit rather than the soil. If we can focus on the soil, however, the fruit will come.

I once did a Bible study with a group of friends where we read a John Eldridge book. I don't know this is the exact quote but it went something like this "Every man must have three things: A battle to fight, an adventure to live, and a woman to save." That quote resonated with me as I thought, "Life is not that simple is it? Sometimes we find ourselves on the losing side of the battle. Sometimes our adventures are filled with anxiety. Sometimes, our drives just push us (and our children) in the wrong direction."

Our body, while complex, needs only a few biological inputs. Our bodies need vitamins, protein, minerals, water, and movement. The human brain is an intricate organ. One part of the brain, the limbic system, can really throw off this delicate machine. The limbic system appears to be primarily responsible for our emotional life, and also has much to do with the formation of our memories.

Part of the limbic system is an organ called the hypothalamus, which is about the size of a thumb tip. The hypothalamus is responsible for regulating your hunger, thirst, response to pain, levels of pleasure, sexual satisfaction, anger, and aggressive behavior. The hypothalamus is the source of our basic drives. When you wonder, "Why do I get so mad at my children on the baseball field?" you can go straight to your hypothalamus for the answer. The emotional state this little organ can create will blind the rest of our brain from rational choices all day long. It is the reason why when you say "no" another voice says you should have said "yes." Acclaimed writer Nigel Calder once said "Had its functions been known in medieval times, the hypothalamus would no doubt have been designated the Devil's playground."

By the way, your hypothalamus is out there on the golf course with you. During a practice round, have you ever wondered why it is so easy to go for a par five in two, but during the tournament it is tough? Have you ever wondered why it is so easy for you to step up and make that four foot putt on the practice green, but on the course your mind starts chattering to you? Have you ever wondered why tournament scores are higher than practice round scores? Sometimes there are no clear answers to questions like these.

The questions above really center on personal growth and mindset. Dr. Clay Parker shared a concept that really helped me think about a possible way to help parents help their children as they grow. He laid the concept out like this:

PROVIDER-COP-COACH-CONSULTANT

In the beginning, we provide for and nurture our children. As they grow older, we become their cop: i.e., "Don't touch the stove!" Later, as they reach their teen years, children want a coach. The parent must become a coach because children in this stage desire "freedom" and a coach must "trust." If a parent is being a cop during this stage, however, the parent can stifle freedom by being commanding. As our children mature, and set out on a life for themselves, they want a wise consultant. They have been coached long enough. Now, they only require help in an occasional decision.

So when I begin to discuss a "Routine" with a junior golfer, it is important for me to understand where both the junior golfer and their parents are from a basic mind set perspective. Are the parents playing "cop" to their 13 year old child? While we were all created similar in terms of parts like brains, muscles, bones, tendons, and ligaments, we definitely are not all be raised the same way. The drive of parents has a tremendously positive (or negative) effect on their children. Generally, the outcome of this drive is mediocrity. Occasionally, however, the outcome of this drive is greatness.

If I were to list some ways for anyone (including your children) to stay on the road to mediocrity, the list would include:

- Eat pasteurized foods
- Drink a lot of sugar-loaded sodas.
- Limit your movement to video games, television, computers, and smart phones.
- Let your brain rule you.
- Give into every indulgence.
- If you feel a need to do it, then do it.
- Be completely outcome oriented.
- Forget the process.
- Live for the moment.

If I were to list some ways to help anyone (including your children) be great, the list would include:

- Eat natural foods.
- Drink a lot of water.
- Begin your day with movement.
- Sustain movement through what we commonly call "exercise" every day.
- Define your goals.
- Ignore any impulse that does not fit into your goals.
- Use emotion on only what you can control.
- Be completely process oriented.
- Forget the outcome.
- Live life over the long run.

The concept that "One day you will get to a crossroad in your life and you must make the right decision." is false. Every single day is a crossroad in our lives. Every single day matters. No wonder we, and our children, are so often "castles made of sand."

So take a stroll with me. Our stroll will end well if you can put some of your pre-conceived thoughts behind you. In addition, try to put some of your regrets behind you. We can't go back and take a different path. But, there is a path ahead that we can take together that leads to genuine learning. Are you up to it?

Who are You?

Introduction.

Are some children more talented than others? If a child shows great potential, what can a coach or parent do to foster it? Should the child specialize or play other sports? Is early specialization in a sport good or bad? This chapter will introduce several key concepts: LTAD, Stages of Development, and Functional Literacy. These concepts will give you an understanding of the importance of movement for your junior golfer. Here you will find clear arguments that early movement is vital to success in later years.

"The central research finding is that no one becomes a world class expert without ten years or more of intense attention to training and practice in the area of expertise. World class experts may be defined as the top few hundred person in any domain: Olympic winners in sports, concert pianists who win international prizes, strong chess Grandmasters, Nobel Prize winners in science, and members of national academies, and the like." (Bloom, 1985; Hayes, 1988)

Herbert Simon won the Nobel Prize in Economics (1978) partly for his research into the role of knowledge in expertise. Mr. Simon coined the phrase: "Overnight Success starts ten years earlier." It was his research that led to many experts in the scientific field to agree on the aspect of a player reaching elite levels of performance after ten years of training.

Subsequent research has debated the familiar "10,000 hour rule" that says it generally takes 10,000 hours of dedicated practice to be able to achieve world-class status in any endeavor. Regardless, the predictions of this research are clear: becoming highly proficient at any endeavor requires training. There is probably not a parent on the face of the earth that does not wish for their children to be elite at something.

If you are wondering if your child is a prodigy let's take a look at some true prodigies. Bobby Fisher won the United States Chess Championship at 14. He became a Grandmaster during the World-Championships qualification cycle at 15 years old. Wayne Gretzky was skating with ten year olds at the age of six. At age ten, he scored 378 goals and had 139 assists, in just 85 games! At the age of six, Willie Mosconi played against professional pool players. Prodigal children cannot be hidden. They will demonstrate their abilities on a national and international level quickly.

For sake of discussion, I have created the following classification categories. Where do you think your child fits?

- **Highly Talented**. Children in this group have accomplishments that do not merit the distinction of a prodigy. Nonetheless, they are competing at a much higher level than other children.

- **Average**. Children in this group are developing in growth, maturation, and physical literacy at the same rate as most children. Obviously, this is, by far, the largest group of children.

- **Below Average**. Children in this group have not developed their physical literacy, have not matured, or have not developed at a traditional rate. Note that if parents keep a perfectly normal child from joining the world of physical literacy, movement, and rules to help them mature, children can easily fall into this group.

- **Challenged**. Children in this group may have a life-altering physical or mental condition.

I have found that, generally, parents bump their children up one class level. The talented one becomes the prodigy. Continuing, the average one becomes the talented one. The below average nine year old child is viewed as an average nine year old. We, as parents, often do not look deeply enough into our children and make an honest assessment of their prowess in a certain area. It is hard to do so. After all, they do go from crawling at two years old to riding a bike at five years old. By age six or so, they are competing in many areas of mental and physical literacy.

Chances are your child is average, unless you have brought them up in an environment where physical and mental literacy has been taught intensely. If that is the case, they may be talented or even demonstrate some prodigal characteristics. How can you be sure, however, that this "ability" continues? How can you be certain this "ability" grows?

"Imagine a man and a woman. Imagine a child and a family with its concentric rings of youthful dreams and mature wisdom. Does a picture come to mind? I'll bet one does, and I'd say it's probably a motion picture." Pete Egoscue, in <u>**The Egoscue Method of Health Through Motion.**</u>

To continue the ability your child exhibits, keep them moving. On the path to stardom are many footsteps. The children must learn as many fundamental movement skills as possible. The children must learn as many fundamental sport skills as possible. Movement is the basic building block of sport and life. Sitting around worrying about how your child is going to fix their backswing should be a low priority. Placing your child in a competitive arena with the goal for them to win should also be a low priority. The fundamental reason for children to compete is to have them move. Heck, simply playing more with other children is movement—often unstructured playing is joyous movement.

People of all ages must move enough to keep their bodies healthy. For a child, they must run, jump, throw, and kick in all directions. Early specialization, such as only swinging a golf club, will almost always cause dysfunction in the muscular/skeletal system. The athlete will work around this dysfunction until they are injured or until they simply hate the sport. What children need is bilateral function. They need movement in every plane of motion.

Emphasis on Multiple Types of Movement.

The emphasis should be put on: awareness (kinesthetic), throwing, kicking, dribbling (and all manner of object manipulation), balance, coordination, speed, changing directions, running, jumping, dodging, skipping, hopping, bounding, and sprinting. Building physical fitness through movement is the reason children should play sports at an early age. These days, physical education has been deeply uprooted from schools. Moreover, these days both parents generally work and the world is simply "a different place" than the world in which you and I grew up. Ipads, Google, and the internet will likely eliminate the need to walk to the library. In short, in today's world, children simply do not get a daily dose of movement. Consequently, their physical literacy is generally low.

Suppose you and your child walk into our Teaching Center. You have the belief that golf is a sport where anyone can become proficient. Your child is ten. You are driven aren't you? You want what is best for your child. You want them to feel the pride that comes with accomplishment. On the other hand, I am not yet emotionally attached to your child. I want them to uncover their physical and mental literacy. We are going to do so through golf. Can you imagine, however, what goes on in my mind when I see a child swing a golf club with no sense of the impending strike of the ball.

I had a player win the US Kids World Championship at age nine. Another one of my students won the Mississippi State Amateur at age 16—the youngest champion in the history of the competition. Are they prodigies? Are they talented? The truth is they both have a high level of competency with fundamental movement skills. In these two examples, their ability to strike, throw, and kick, for example, is so good that breaking through the "proficiency barrier" of winning a golf tournament is highly likely. Without their competency in fundamental movements, I really doubt whether either of them would ever win such a golf tournament.

We will all look at our children and ask, "Who are you"? Sometimes we ask this in a negative sense and sometimes in a positive sense. When you are motivated by a compulsion to help your children, however, I urge you to select **movement** first. Stay away from the definitions of talented or average or below average. It is evident to me that children that move in multiple planes of motion versus children that do not move will be deemed more talented.

We are driven to perform for a desire outcome. The problem is we seldom look into the process of the outcome. The process of fundamental movement skills or physical literacy should be the **first place** you go to help your child with any sport. In other words, you do not have to worry about what sport they should play. Instead, worry about the daily dose of movement your children receive. Remember, if you want to change the outcome, you must change the process. As in the Biblical parable, you must add fertilizer to the soil if you expect the tree to bear fruit.

Sports such as table tennis, dart throwing, Frisbee, and racquetball train the wrists both in speed and accuracy. Wrist release patterns are basically subconscious or automatic responses. As a result, playing these sports will definitely enhance chipping, pitching, and clubface control.

Sports such as baseball, football, basketball, discus, and javelin will train children to generate power and accuracy. Sports such as soccer, martial arts, boxing, or volleyball will teach striking. Proficiency at striking a golf ball, for example combine the ability to create force from the ground (i.e., throwing) and the ability to deliver a strike (i.e., boxing).

Golf is a sport of both power and geometry. Tennis and baseball are other sports in which players strike an object with an implement. Traditionally, tennis players catch onto golf more quickly than baseball players for two reasons. First, the striking weight shift in tennis is like the striking weight shift in golf. Note that the striking weight shift in baseball differs from the weight shifts in tennis and golf. Also, a tennis racket has a face, like a golf club, so the player can affect the ball flight. But, hitting a round object with another round object certainly improves eye hand coordination.

"Kids who have fun playing a sport are more likely to stay active and healthy for their entire lifetime. They also have a better chance of becoming a top athlete. So make it fun, and make it quality." Canadian Sport Centres

Growth Velocities.

Even though your child might not have an obvious physical challenge, there is an important lesson here. Have you noticed children growing at different rates? Peak Growth Velocity is the maximum rate of growth that occurs during the pubertal growth spurt. During a child's development, there will be growth velocities and these velocities can offer windows of opportunity for children to learn or give them fits. When the children's bodies begin to grow, their growth generally means they will be dysfunctional. Their body cannot function according to its natural design. The bones, muscles, tendons, and ligaments do not grow at the same time. The children will adjust to these differences on a sub-conscious level.

These growth velocities often make it difficult to assess talent. Early development, or early growth velocities, generally leads to a lack of coordination. As the child gets acclimated to the growing bones and changing muscles they are often overshadowed by the late developing children. Consequently, a parent or coach mistakes a lack of coordination or speed with early developmental growth. Sometimes early development leads to a labeling of "she is your basketball player," or "he is your golfer." In truth, development, whether early or late, has its pros and cons. The early developer will have a physical advantage in the short run. The late developer has a better chance of creating a great work ethic in the long run.

I call another factor that hinders talent assessment, "societal complexity." Physical literacy can be defined as the development of movement skills and sport skills. Children that are raised in a society of movement will gain physical literacy. Children raised in a society of knowledge will gain communication literacy—they will gain reading and writing skills.

The task of defining talent is difficult. Is the child talented? Or, are their growth, maturation, and society better suited for whatever it is we call "talent?"

Another, more subtle, hindrance to assessing talent is the fact that there are different types of sports. There are early specialization sports such as gymnastics and figure skating. Early specialized sports can be defined as a sport in which the player will be retiring at 14 to 16 years of age. If your child wants to win an Olympic gold medal, early specialization in gymnastics is critical. Beginning to flip around at age 17 just will not do the trick.

There are late specialization sports such as football and golf. Late specialized sports can be defined as a sport where full potential is not met until after full growth maturity. When entering these different types of sporting events the "definition" of talent, prodigy, or average will obviously change.

The young stars of today, like Venus and Serena Williams (or Tiger Woods), have led many parents to believe that their child should also specialize early. Perhaps this conclusion is valid. But the vast majority of children will not have the physiological or psychological function to merit early specialization.

Dysfunction.

In this context, I define "dysfunction" as the inability of the body to function according to its design. I define "compensation" as what the body substitutes when dysfunction is present. So, depending on your child's goal, they could be physically inhibited because of necessary compensations created in response to various dysfunctions. The quickest way for a child to become dysfunctional is to be consistently dormant. That is, they do not exhibit movement in any plane of motion, and continue to fail to exhibit movement.

When our children move, it is not simple movement that causes pain or injuries. Pain or injuries occur because muscles that were never intended to be used for a particular motion are called in to make up for the dysfunctional muscles. The muscle and skeletal systems are designed for movement. As children go through various growth velocities, however, they may have a little trouble "talking to these muscles." In effect, we are all inhibited, or at least dysfunctional, as we grow. All children will go through cycles of dysfunction.

In fact, all of us are prone to injury through lack of movement. We can all feel dysfunctions, or at least compensations, every morning as we celebrate our 40th or 50th birthday. You might know someone in these age classes who complain of aching shoulders, hips, or lower backs.

Istvan Balyi developed the long-term athletic development model in 1990. In this model, Balyi points out there is a "variability to trainability." The child will pick up on movement at different rates depending on the child's competence in functional movement, where they are in their growth velocity, and the drill or exercise they are doing. In this way, placing a child in a box labeled talented, average, or below average becomes even more incorrect. It is likely what we deem talented is simply being asymptomatic functionally, having a foundation of movement (parents), and having unknowingly been cross-training with movement. Talent could simply be function in a world of dysfunction!

At one time, I was deemed to be a talented boxer. After getting in a fight on the school bus when I was nine years old, my father took me to the local boxing club. The coach could not believe how quickly I got the foot work and the movement around the ring. My punching style needed some help, but he told my father I was a "natural." You and I can probably imagine the pride my father felt. Behind the scenes, however, I was a very avid soccer and tennis player. Footwork and ball handling skills were a part of my life already, so moving around a ring to keep from getting hit came pretty easily to me. I was stamped as "talented" and in the beginning that really helped. I won fights, believed in myself, and my self-image grew. At the national level it was a bit different; as evidenced by my curved nose to prove. Was it that I was really less talented than the best boxers or was it something else?

LTAD Stages.

You probably have similar stories. You go from a beginner to really good in a short time. It is as if there is no time table for you. You were talented! A Natural! Maybe your children are doing the same thing. Before we label them, however, let's look at an LTAD's stages of development. Have your children had the opportunity to gain functional literacy as they grew?

- **An Active Start** is the first stage. It is from birth to age six that children are highly involved in daily active play. Running around, jumping over walls, and tripping over the bicycle are keys to professional sports for a three year old. The fundamentals movement skills and physical literacy skills are bred here. Movement milestones such as balancing on one foot, hopping on one foot, catching a bounced ball, and heel to toe walking are important.

- **FUNdamentals is** the second phase of development. This phase is from age six to eight for girls and age six to nine for boys. Here, agility, balance, coordination and speed are learned. The focus in this stage is on fun when learning the fundamentals of movement skills. A variety of sports and physical activities should be stressed and formal competition should be minimized.

- **Learning to Train** is the "Golden Age of Learning." In this stage, their fundamental sport skills are built from their fundamental movement skills. The children are ready for formalized methods with a number of activities. In this stage, girls are 8 to 11 years old, and the boys are 9 to 12 years old. In this stage, it will be tempting to specialize in terms of a specific sport or even a particular position in a sport. Premature specialization, however, will not promote by-lateral movement and will increase the likelihood of injury.

- **Train to Train** is for the 11 to 15 year old female and the 12 to 16 year old male. This stage will "make or break" the athlete. Some will show special talents and true interest in the sport. Nonetheless, there should still be considerable time spent on training skills and general physical fitness. In this stage, time should be divided half to training and half to competition.

- **Train to Compete** is for the 15 to 21 year old female and the 16 to 23 year old male. This is the "serious" stage of athletic development. These athletes are committed and are generally known as "aspiring" athletes. These children have recognized their talent and are generally committed to one sport. In this stage, we find high levels of competition, nutrition, sport performance training, and exercise.

- **Train to Win** is the final stage of performance. In this stage, there are big trophies to be had and the athletes are now pursuing their sport full time. They train to maintain and maximize their performance. For girls, this stage begins at age 18 and for boys this stage begins at age 19.

- **Active for Life** is the final stage. Maybe **Train to Train** didn't work out as planned. Still, the athlete has a great base for activity all their life.

What do we parents do, however? When our children are in the 11 to 15 age bracket, many of us parents are on an active hunt for a sport for our children to play. The children in this age group, however, do not have a great physical base built. We think that these children need to engage in something seriously. So, we take them to the best coaches we can find and push them to become competitive. We are just praying they will "get it" so they can get a college scholarship or, at least, have something to showcase their talents.

Let's read the quote at the beginning of the chapter once again:

> *"The central research finding is that no one becomes a world class expert without ten years or more of intense attention to training and practice in the area of expertise. World class experts may be defined as the top few hundred person in any domain: Olympic winners in sports, concert pianists who win international prizes, strong chess Grandmasters, Nobel Prize winners in science, and members of national academies, and the like." (Bloom, 1985; Hayes, 1988)*

Whether it is exactly 10,000 hours or ten years of instense training, it will take an enormous amount of work to be world class at any endeavor. In addition, for children, I believe it also takes a great base of fundamental movement skills and fundamental multi-sport skills. Movement will help our children build their athleticism with function—not working around dysfunction.

Golf is a PGA Professional's passion. They strive to give children the best opportunities to become as good as they wish to be. Consequently, when a youngster stands in front of me and starts talking about ball flight or what their right hand is doing, I am not really listening. I am watching them move. I am learning about their fundamental movement skills. I am learning about their past experiences as a human. I am figuring out how their parents were driven and how they drove them.

A sense of reason and logic must come to mind here. From birth to age six, before air conditioning, 120 cable channels, and video games, kids were moving. Agility, balance, coordination, and speed were learned as kids road bikes, played kick the can, jumped over ditches, and walked across fallen trees. At about age nine, most children or parents were not worried about travel teams or college sports. Pick up games of baseball, soccer, football, and golf were created by the children. After all, why come inside the house? There was nothing to do! At about age 11, mom and dad could not take them everywhere, so the children began to carve their own paths in sports. By age 16 or 17, everyone knew how good they were.

Times are different now. College football (one of my favorite sports) is more like a theatrical act than the game "Rudy" played. People return in droves to their alma mater to re-visted old memories or to share new ones. The parents and the kids look at the excitement around them. The kid is in….all in. He wants to play here! Now mom and dad have been busy, and the child is already nine years old. Video games and the Disney channel are more the norm than riding a bike seven miles a day. This is a sticky situation.

Often times PGA Professionals are on the other end of this "stickiness." The child and the parents are now ready for competition. It is time to pave their road to college. Often times, I remind them that climbing the ladder from learning to play to learning to compete takes time. In fact, this subject is the focus of a later chapter.

The point here is that we simply ***must get out of the habit of placing children in the box of talented or average or below average***. Physical literacy is learned just like reading or writing or arithmetic. You and I must be driven to excel at the ***process*** of helping our children grow their physical literacy. The ***process is primary.***

The first step in the process is to get children moving. The process does not begin by teaching your child to keep their head down when hitting a driver or expecting a win in the junior golf tournament. At age seven, eight, or even ten, the process is all about movement. That is, which team your child plays on, or if they make the "select" team or trophies are not important to the process. Movement, however, forms the base of the process.

If you find yourself being angry or frustrated because your son or daughter is losing golf tournaments at age ten, then you are not involved in the process. I am sorry to tell you that. There is nothing wrong with you. Before you get too deeply invested into pushing your son or daughter into full time instruction (or ten tournaments each year), look into their movement.

If you find that your children have not followed the "perfect" model of fundamental movement skills, then join the club. Very few people have. So do not waste your time over what has passed. Karate, Boxing, Tennis, and Soccer are great sports that cross train golf. If your young child has not participated in these cross training sports, do not despair. Another big growth velocity, where your children will have a really great chance of picking up all types of motion through training, occurs around puberty.

Entertain ideas of the process and functional movement literacy. Entertain the idea of multiple sports that are not necessarily for competition. So what if the coach keeps moving my seven year old from goalie to forward? So what if the coach keeps moving your son from 1st base to the outfield? So what if my son gets outrun or outkicked? So what? They are learning, just like the rest of us. Keep them busy with movement and the dividends will be great. Just make sure the movement is in all directions.

In terms of golf, the worst idea for your child is to go to a driving range and hit golf balls for two hours a day. It does not matter if they are being coached or instructed for the entire two hours. I don't care. Simple ball pounding is a terrible idea. Get the children instruction, sure, but get them on the course. Let them play. Don't worry so much about their swings. Tell them to hit it the golf ball hard at a young age. Keep their clubs short and do not let them get bored on the course.

If your child is older, say in puberty, keep them playing multiple sports. You might fear that they will be injured in other sports. But, keep in mind, however, that keeping them out of other sports has a dramatic negative effect on the sport in which they might specialize. Here in the South, we think there are two sports: football and spring football. But, your child does not have to play football to increase their range of motion. Activities like karate or Parisi

Speed School or some other "non-specific" sport helps your child move in in multiple planes.

Yoga, Egoscue, and Pilates might not be favorite activities for your sons and daughters. They are, however, great for getting the body moving in different planes. By-lateral disfunctions are bound to happen when the body moves in a limited number of directions. Postural Analysis or TPI screens are useful because the human body is a bilateral machine. It should be monitored so that it can remain at its functional peak, wherever that might be. Think of it like this. **Who would possibly think that eliminating mobility from a child's workout is a brilliant idea?**

I have taught two children that specialized much too quickly. Sadly, it was my fault. Both went to small private schools. Historically, these schools have produced athletes that could not compete at the Division I level. I pushed them to specialize at golf—with mixed results. One student burned out by 16, but eventually came back to the game and is now playing at a Division II school. The other was offered golf scholarships, but not at the school he wanted. He went on to be a leader in student government and will soon receive his undergraduate degree.

The reason I am sharing this story with you is because it is easy to remove, or reduce, movement and insert, or increase, specialization. Fundamental movement skills form the base for specialzation. I believe that children should not specialize in a sport until they are 16 years old or older. That doesn't mean they can't love a certain sport—it just means they must move in multiple planes. Invest in your children through movement. The dividends for them will be great.

Let me explain why I focus on movement. When children come in for golf lessons there are generally "compensations" from a "dysfunctional" golf swing. By this I mean the golf swing will have tendencies that will not be advantageous through the bag. My job is to alter these tendencies. Identifying the compensation in the swing is easy, identifying the compensation in the child's life is difficult. By getting your children involved in movement (in multiple planes which generally means multiple sports) early and keeping them involved, you will be doing more good than any golf lesson could!

The purpose of these multiple sports and activities is for movement, not to win trophies. If the only reason you have your child in gymnastics is to win trophies, I think your reason is faulty. There is a lot to becoming a champion. There is a lot to learn. At every sport's core there is one necessity though—movement! Get the kids moving and keep them moving!

Chapter Lessons:

- It is going to take many years of intense training to reach elite levels of performance.
- Understand the competency level of your children in fundamental movements, but do not put them in a box of "talented" or "average."
- The body requires movement for health.
- Play multiple sports to cross train your children.
- Do not focus on winning when your children are young—focus on movement.
- There are seven developemental stages. To become good takes time.
- They are your children, so keep them moving in as many directions as possible.

INSIGHTS

I conducted a series of interviews during the winter of 2011. Note that I have not revealed the identities of the people being interviewed. If you really have to know who this person is, there are plenty of tips given so that, if you do a little digging, you will be able to figure it out. *His father's insights are in italicized text.*

I met this individual in 2007. My first impression of him was that he was very happy in his own skin. He had goals that he believed he could accomplish and, after spending some time with him, I came to believe that he could. He is presently a member of the PGA Tour, with winnings in excess of three million dollars in the past two years. His story is just beginning.

"How many sports did you play as a child?"

"VJ, I played all of them. I played soccer, basketball, football, etc. You name it and I played them."

"He played them all, Soccer, baseball, football, basketball, etc. Basketball was his first love. QB of football team—you name it; he played it. We probably spent untold hours in the backyard throwing balls to one another."

"When did you start playing golf?"

"Well, my Dad says he put a club in my hand as soon as I could walk. My father was in the military and I can remember hitting balls with him on base. We had to shag our own balls, so there weren't any practice facilities per se. I can say my dad never took me kicking and screaming to the golf course. We would go play with other dads and their kids.

"I remember this one family we would play with in Nebraska. It was a father and two sons. The oldest of the brothers had a bunch of talent, but was really burned out on the sport. The youngest loved the game but didn't have the talent. One day when the five of us were playing, I three putted one hole and Dad really rode me hard. The other dad took my dad off to the side and said something to him that must have made a real difference because after that there was never too much riding me from my father."

"I stuck a club in his hands when he was in diapers. He gripped it cross-handed in the beginning. Sometime between 6 and 8 he moved to a

conventional grip. He was always around me, kind of like a shadow. I played other sports with him but if he wanted to play golf I was Johnny on the Spot. When he was 13 or 14, I stopped playing golf with my buddies and started playing with him. We would play nine holes every day of the week and 18 or 27 each day on the weekend.

"A defining moment happened when he was in Nebraska. Dean Wilson was a six or seven time State Amateur Champion. We would play nine holes with him on some evenings. My son had chipped on the green and three putted. I was chewing his butt. Dean grabbed me by my shoulder and put his finger in my face saying, 'Don't you screw your child up the way I did mine with this game.' I can't tell you how many times I didn't get onto him because of this advice."

"When did golf become the sport?"

"Golf became the sport when I was 12 or 14 I guess. I got hit hard by a pitch in baseball and couldn't seem to stay in the batter's box the way I wanted to after that. Growth stopping at 5'10" ended my dream of starting at North Carolina (ed. in basketball). I can remember living in Montana and shoveling snow away so that I could work on my jump shots. But because I never got taller, I began to turn toward golf."

"But was there a moment when you said to yourself, 'Hey this is something I can do?'"

"I guess you could say losing to Tim Burnett at 13. I realized the reason I lost was because he was a more developed golf wise. All he did was play golf, so his skill set was better than mine. He worked harder at golf than I did, but it took him 19 or 20 holes to get rid of me. He was the top seed in the match play event and I was the last qualifier."

"You have to remember at this time I was still the starting quarterback also. My team wasn't very good. Basketball was my love—but, I wasn't growing. I loved baseball but it just seemed like golf was easy for me."

"My dad always emphasized that golf was an individual sport. I have always worked hard at every sport I ever played and sometimes it rubbed me the wrong way when other guys didn't. I have always been a student of every sport I played. I felt technique and form was very important in how you played sports. I spent all my winter with split fingers because I would try and shoot the basketball from my fingertips. I can remember going to school, checking out books on pool and learning to put spin on the cue ball. Stuff like that."

"He was a highly motivated kid, learning as he played. He won the central Alabama high school state championship his junior or senior year. Him, Stewart Cink, and Brian Gay were all the same age. So with the motivation to beat them combined with a desire to learn would be when I think golf really became the sport for him."

"Did you check out books on all the sports?"

"I didn't check out books on golf because of my Dad. He was very protective on who gave me advice. I still have a thirst for knowledge in things that interest me."

"Was your practice as deliberate in golf as it sounds like it was in basketball?"

"Whether it was deliberate practice or not, I wanted to do it the right way. To be good at something you must understand how to do it. Everyone does it a certain way. If you are not doing it as well as you want to, you are not doing something efficient enough. I always tried to find those keys. I can remember throwing footballs in my back yard and trying to get the nose of the ball to turn over and drop. I would change my grip to get it to spin the way I wanted. I guess I was watching ball flight with a football!"

"At the end of the day, I guess that is why I am sometimes critical of other athletes. I spent a lot of time trying to be great at multiple sports. I am not an expert at everything but I see people trying to be great and not working on it perfectly. What do they expect?"

"Did you ever receive instruction?"

"I always had a simple swing. My dad was a phenomenal golfer. He would go all summer without ever shooting in the 70's. He always broke 70! My dad was probably my instructor until my freshman year in college. By then I had gotten it to the point where I could make adjustments on the fly and change things."

"I too was a typical 16 or 17 year old and always tried to hit it perfect. That is a tough age because you always want to hit it perfect. By college I had pretty much figured out you don't have to hit it perfect to play great golf. After my freshman year in college my parents moved to DC. My Dad took me to see Bill Strausbaugh. He told us he only taught members and tour players. My Dad being my Dad, he took me anyway."

"I remember him saying no at first but then I somehow hit a ball in front of him and he said he could work with me at 10:00 the following day. To this day I don't do any of what he taught me but he was somebody my Dad trusted with his son. I saw him one or two times each summer and he was always very complimentary of me."

"When he was 14 or 15 we came to an agreement that I would not help him unless he asked. I didn't teach him a lot about swinging a club, but I told him to 'put his hands on it and hit is as hard as you can.' I kept people away from him because he didn't need a lot of work on his swing. Some people nowadays teach ten points in the swing but we didn't do that. We played. I emphasized the short game to him. Probably the thing I taught him was how to hit a variety of shots from ten yards and in. He picked up balls for $1 hour at a driving range. His mom would tell him she would pay him a dollar not to go to the range because it took her 40 minutes to drive there. He would chip and putt until his mom showed up after he would call for a ride home. He never hooked it because we emphasized hitting it hard. That is where his turn through the ball came from."

"Can you define your practice over the years? Tell us how you went about it?"

"I have never stood on a range and beat balls. I don't think I ever beat balls. A lot of time when I would practice I would be playing. I spent some time in the golf business after school and I remember thumbing through a book that had thirty of the best players' swings frame by frame. There were only two that didn't have their shoulders turned basically 90 degrees when their lead arms were parallel to the ground. That became a key for me that I still use today."

"Now I have gotten big into reps in my practice. On the range I will hit more wedge through 7 irons than anyone on tour. I base how I am hitting it on the seven, eight, and nine irons. That way, on the course, I know that I am good at it and it will be second nature. I don't even think about hitting an 8 iron to a back right pin. I just hit it."

"A lot of the reason I developed this is because they are the clubs that are easy to hit and you don't feel like an idiot when you don't hit it perfect. Wedges ten feet off get me pissed in practice. Un-solid three irons piss me off. I will hit so many eight and nine irons that sometimes I have to rush to hit drivers before going to the first tee. I am also aware that a missed four iron or hybrid can kill my mojo during a practice session. If I can hit the eight iron on the button I know that I am swinging well. Right now I am not looking for perfection, I just want every shot I hit to be quality. That is what aggravates me sometimes with the putter. I want quality and proficiency through the bag."

"Over the years I have watched other players hit long irons and get amazed how many poor shots were coming out. I just don't think that is intelligent. To me the feel of a well struck golf shot and watching it fly is pretty euphoric. So you fall in love with a feeling and you just keep going with it. For me it is something I love to do. On the course with a seven iron to wedge I am completely confident. Point and Click."

"There was nobody in particular that he watched. He didn't do drills at home or on the range. Ball striking was important but learning to play was more important. I don't ever recall a drill ever done at home. We just played together and when he went off to college I had a hard time because my playmate was gone."

"In the 1970's I was playing mini tours some. Frank Conner never finished worse than 3rd and was even better when he was playing for his own money. I still remember a day when eight or ten of us were in the locker room and somebody said, 'How did you play?' I said '18 greens and shot 70.' I didn't quit that day but it was the catalyst from me finding something else to do."

"My boy got ignited somewhere along the way. I can remember telling him he needed a back-up plan in case he didn't play the PGA Tour. He said he was going to play the tour. You have to remember he went to 11 different schools before finishing high school because of my job. He was highly motivated to beat his dad."

"Do you think you have put 10,000 hours of deliberate practice in with your golf game?"

"When I was a club pro, I would practice for one and one-half hours and play. Factoring the amount of time I have played golf I would suggest it could hit that number easily. One thing I have always been very good at is getting something out of my practice. I don't waste effort. I have maximized my time by not over working or over analyzing what I am doing. I have had practice sessions that last fifteen or twenty minutes that are great. On tour it happens a lot. If I can't focus, I don't just go to the range and beat balls. I never have. The focus of the practice for me is always primary. If my mind is wandering, then it is impossible for me to get anything out of practice."

"I always wanted to figure out the answers for myself. I know when I should stop practicing. I also know when I am focusing. If I am playing a little too passively, or something like that, I will not go beat balls. That is when I go home and look in the mirror and have a little heart to heart with myself. You have to find the courage to keep getting better."

"Ten thousand hours of practice. Well, he grew up on the golf course. I don't know how many years it takes to get to ten thousand hours. I didn't want him hitting balls with full clubs un-supervised. So he would just warm up and go the golf course. If he were practicing, the bulk of it would be short game. He did most of that himself. I would ask him questions like if this ball is sitting down what is going to happen? He would then hit it and we would learn together. I would say things like 'the ball is in this position, this is what you could do' and we would build a lab. If he was having a problem with his swing we could fix it in ten swings.

"At what point did golf become instinct?"

"VJ. Golf has always been instinct for me. Everyone gets the rules, but the guys that are good at it are thinking one shot ahead. It is similar to pool. Even though you are focusing on the shot at hand, you're focusing on where it will leave you. The nuances of golf are hard to teach. This is why some college and junior golfers have perfect motions but can't be elite. Golf is instinctual when you are ever evolving and adapting to situations without thinking about them. That stuff can't be taught. It has to be learned. Whether it was watching my dad play, or just playing a bunch as a kid, I learned it. It was just instinct."

"I don't know. I would always tell him 'You must control yourself before you can control the ball.' Whether it is combat, work, golf or whatever there is a rush that comes over your body. Nobody can see it but it is there. How you make decisions during this phase makes all the difference. So I probably talked to him more over the years about controlling the emotions more than anything else. "

Notable Achievements:

- **Turned pro 1995**
- **Winner on Nationwide Tour 2008**
- **2 runner-up finishes on PGA Tour**
- **Chosen as 1 of the TOP 100 to watch on PGA Tour 2012**

Underwater BB Stacking

Introduction.

Practice. What is it? Why is it that some people build great golf motions but most cannot? Why do most golfers only experience frustration when they practice? This chapter introduces several key concepts: Deliberate Practice, The 70/30 rule, Testing versus Practicing, and "Noisy" feedback. These concepts will serve you well as your junior golfer grows in the game. These concepts give you the ability to discuss the "reasons" behind spending hours at the golf course. That is, why are you at the golf course? Are you there to test your skills? Are you there to build a better motion? Are you spending too much time "testing" instead of practicing? It is important to have a frame of reference for being at the golf course.

Three Stages of Practice.

Practice, like nearly every movement, decision, or motivation goes through three stages.

- The first stage is anticipation. For example, anticipation can happen when you are going to a baseball game, when you meeting someone new, or just heading home after work. We always anticipate that which we are aware of happening in the future.

- The second stage is action. So now we are in the middle of it. We are experiencing the ball game, are looking the person in the eye, or we are with our family at home.

- The third stage is reinforcement. The action is over. Did the ball game end the way we wanted? Was it fun? Did the new person seem kind or interesting? Did the family have a good evening? What problems were there to solve? What funny thing happened?

The power of these three stages is what makes practice so important and so difficult to understand. Everyone goes out to the lesson tee anticipating something. During the action phase, they are working on something. As they walk away from the practice area, they are re-enforcing something. The same stages occur on the golf course. The same stages happen during competition.

Disappointment during the action phase is generally the reason golfers come to our Teaching Center. My clients want only one thing—to become better golfers. They want their golf ball to fly more often in the direction they are intending. Many of my new clients seem to believe that I will say something to them or simply give them a feeling that will instantly fix their ball flight. This belief is simply incorrect. I have no magic words. I can't give someone a feeling. I can, however, tell them the exact area where they can change a feeling. The feeling that they build for themselves depends on how they practice.

No Thinking and Swinging.

I suggest that, more than anything, people are held back at this sport because they "think they can think" during their swing. Unfortunately, nothing is further from the truth. As you will learn in this chapter, the brain, muscles, and skeletal system have rules that govern how well they perform together. It is not just the brain or the muscles. It is the whole package—down to the ligaments and tendons and beyond. So, if you want to learn something right now, learn this: **Stop Teaching Yourself to Think about Your Swing While You Are Hitting a Golf Ball**.

When I was a youngster, my dad, Vic Trolio, said something I will never forget: "VJ Trolio, you are going to be great at something, even if it is underwater bb stacking!" I have had 30 years to build a visual of "underwater bb stacking." So for just a moment think about it. I don't know where my dad came up with this, (he is famous for his off-the-cuff sayings) but it gives a great visual of what practice should be.

Practice should be tougher than competition. Practice should have a single focus. Practice should build on top of a base (and that base is movement). Practice should be deliberate. Practice should reinforce proper movements. Practice should build proper movements.

"It's a miracle that the modern methods of instruction have not entirely strangled all curiosity of inquiry." —Albert Einstein

The Place to Practice: Think Ben Hogan and Bobby Jones.

One of the biggest problem areas in becoming better at golf is that people generally believe the place to practice is a driving range. The modern method of standing on a driving range and beating balls is critically flawed.

Driving ranges are profit centers and fun places. Driving ranges are easier than the golf course. Driving ranges get your mind on ball flight and your swing. Driving ranges often disguise your flaws and lead to re-enforcement of improper movements.

Mr. Ben Hogan was widely known for practicing. People still speak of the way Mr. Hogan "dug it out of the dirt." People really do not know the whole story. Mr. Hogan went broke twice before being successful at golf. He would become famous for his victories and his intentional practice sessions. Before becoming famous, however, he was just another golfer. Mr. Hogan did not become a champion by practicing at a driving range. However, Mr. Hogan was infamous for practicing at what is called "The Little Nine" at his home club, Shady Oaks. I have been there and I will tell you that it is very different place than a typical driving range. There are all types of elevation changes. All types of slopes are there. Large oak trees line the Little Nine on both sides—which easily simulate a hole. There are multiple targets. Bottom line: The Little Nine is definitely NOT a driving range.

A look into Mr. Hogan's early years and practice sheds light on his ideas of how to get better at golf. First, understand that Mr. Hogan had "Hennie Bogan" who had "an insatiable desire to practice and a greater golfer even than the great Bobby Jones." Hennie was a make believe character that told Mr. Hogan to practice. Moreover, Mr. Hogan did not have access to hundreds of golf balls. He only had what would fit in a shag bag. As a kid, Mr. Hogan jumped on the course with a group of kids and played. He got his start as a caddy; standing beside his "loop" and watching them swing.

How many children caddy these days? How many shag golf balls for themselves? How many are hitting toward a human (generally a caddy) standing in the middle of a field? How many are jumping on the course with a group of children and playing? Finally, how many have an imaginary player, better than even the great Bobby Jones, standing next to them judging their work and shot? Doesn't the word "deliberate" come to mind when you read this account of Mr. Hogan's practice?

Because Mr. Hogan held Mr. Bobby Jones in such high esteem, let's take our own look at Bobby Jones. It seems someone cut down a "cleek" when Bobby was about five years old. Before this, as the story goes, Bobby was trying to wield a club which was much too big for him. After getting his "new" club, Bobby and a friend (they were five years old) laid out a golf course in the front yard. They played the golf course as a daily event. There was no instruction or advice other than: Play the ball as it lies and all strikes count.

The Jones family moved to East Lake because of young Bobby's medical condition. The young Jones found Stewart Maiden, a Scottish player that was the resident professional of East Lake Golf Club. Young Bobby began following Stewart around the course, watching his every move. Before Bobby was seven, he was given permission to play except on Saturdays and Sundays. After school, when he couldn't play, he would practice on the thirteenth green which sat behind his house. He chipped the ball up and putted until the ball was holed. "Pitch to the green and then putt out, pitch to the green and putt out." Does the phrase "deliberate versus mindless" come to mind?

Interestingly enough, both Ben Hogan and Bobby Jones had golf course rivals. Jones had Perry Adair and Hogan had Byron Nelson. These sets of rivals shared competitions on the course. They were playing golf and trying to win.

The Form of Practice in Today's World.

Practice today is far different, isn't it? The parent drops the child off at the course. There, they probably meet a group of friends at the driving range. They hit shots, concerned more with who hits it further and who can to hit the range picker. Soon bored, they go in and grab something to eat. Then, they are off to the pool or to the break room. They are not out watching the best players play. They spend much more time at the practice area than getting out on the course. A day of this is often deemed to be practice. After all, the child spent nearly three hours hitting shots, chipping, and putting.

Let's look at golf instruction. Lessons come at an early age and are mostly given at the driving range. The kids are told, or it is implied, that the driving range is where one comes to practice. They are taught, usually through words, to do this or that with their swings. They are taught to think about their swings and judge ball flight. Albert Einstein was right! Most modern practice programs and facilities stifle the chance of learning.

> *"Self-education is the only real education that there is. Schools and instruction advice can only make self-education easier. Beyond that, they do little."* ---Isaac Asimov

Watching and Deliberate Practice.

Bobby Jones and Ben Hogan watched. They watched players. They used their eyes to learn. Jones and Hogan played the game. They got on the course—or they built courses. Jones and Hogan worked deliberately on their game. Although they educated themselves, they did it deliberately. Whether it was the young Jones glaring at Stewart Maiden's swing or the young Hogan being coached by Hennie, it was deliberate.

Here is the definition of Deliberate Practice: "**Being engaged in activities specifically designed to improve performance with full concentration. It is daily practice done in a work-like manner with a specific goal of improving performance. Moreover, Deliberate Practice, requires high levels of effort and attention and is frequently not enjoyable.**"

Is it easier to dump out 20 balls and chip them or to do as the young Bobby Jones did and pitch one ball and putt it out? Is it easier to stand on the range and hit 50 balls without a target or to have twenty balls that you must pick up yourself as Mr. Hogan did?

Getting better always comes back to the same thing: deliberation in practice. Great junior golfers are deliberate. They enter the practice session with the anticipation of accomplishing a single task. During the action phase of their deliberate practice, they accomplish this task. The re-enforcement comes from seeing the process and creating the outcome they desire. Great juniors do it every day—except on Sunday, of course. Our juniors practice mostly at home, away from the driving range. They do it where they can see themselves do it and for a defined amount of time. Instruction points them in a direction and the students self-educate.

My junior golfers that struggle do not practice each day. In fact, they practice more before a tournament—which is the opposite of what one should do. The focus of their sessions is not on a single task. The action phase gets lost because of poor shots, an undefined session, or someone talking to them. The excuses never end. Because the action phase is not defined, their re-enforcement is not clear. They get lost in the many variables that can affect practice. In effect, they are not practicing—they are taking tests on how well they are controlling their ball. The only problem is, however, that they have not studied for these tests.

Why is it that some junior golfers can stick to the process and some seemingly cannot? From my research, the difference stems from the ability or inability to control emotions during a practice session. It starts early, as you probably know. We all have memories of our children wailing, with tears pouring from their eyes, because they couldn't have a five-cent sucker. From the beginning, it is very easy to get emotional when things aren't going in our favor. This same behavior, while maybe not as dramatic, can be seen all around the world from children on the driving range.

The Effects of Practicing Mindlessly.

I will go out on a limb here and suggest that parents to the aspiring golfer can either help their children or hurt their children when it comes to practice. By this, I mean a parent can either re-enforce their **child's practice habits** or the **outcome of the child's practice habits**. I am speaking of a session on a driving range, not a tournament. There are certainly times when the outcome of a process, such as a scoring slump or a constant bogey finish, must be looked at. The danger lies in when the parent becomes emotionally hijacked by the flight of the ball on the driving range. That teaches the child, well, to act like a child.

Deliberate practice is a simply different. It stands as a dividing line between taking control of the things you can control and accepting the things you cannot control. Deliberate practice uses as many senses as possible to learn. Deliberate practice minimizes variables and maximizes learning. Deliberate practice is defined. In a sense, deliberate practice gets rid of frustration while building motion.

As a youngster, I experienced the effects of practice that was not deliberate. The first time I experienced these effects occurred after the USGA Junior. I made the cut but noticed a need for enhanced ball striking. At the time, Nick Faldo was atop the world. So I took his book to the range and opened it up. There were lots of pictures and drills to follow and I worked hard for the majority of the fall and winter. By spring, however, I was worse. It was not because Faldo was wrong. It was because I messed up in the anticipation phase.

I had no golf instructor. Further, I did not understand how boggled the anticipation phase was in my mind. At the time, I was convinced that a swing could be found. Just a feeling and click, you are on your way. Every time I did one of the drills my concentration was more on the outcome of the shot (while I was doing the drill) than the movement itself. All my work took place at the driving range. There were no mirrors, no video, and most importantly, no separation between the drill and ball flight.

To get out of my slump, I just went back to playing golf. I was a self-pronounced "player" that simply did not benefit from instruction or drills. I experienced these same series of events after my freshman year at Southern Miss. I had made every tournament as a freshman but, because the team was going to be young my second year, Coach Sam Hall red-shirted me. Back to the range I went, this time with even more golf balls! As a youngster, I had to shag balls myself. Now that I was in college, I had access to a 55-gallon drum full of golf balls every day. Of course, history repeated itself. In reflection, I believe that was the worst period in my golf life—trying hard to get better but getting worse.

The Building Blocks of Deliberate Practice.

Learning begins in the anticipation phase. Building a swing or a stroke simply takes time. Your son or daughter will not just "find it." They will build it deliberately one day at a time. They should anticipate the fact that they are getting one percent better each day. They should anticipate that their motion is changing day by day. They should also anticipate working on it each day for a certain amount of time.

There is no evidence to support the idea that hard work in the beginning allows your junior golfer to coast into the future. The game of golf is a tendency of sorts and the body, as we now know, is ever changing. While there are some experts that might put in deliberate practice of three to five hours daily, your child should not be pushed to do this. I always suggest five minutes a day, or possibly thirty repetitions a day, 300 days each year.

While performing deliberate practice, your children need to learn to Look, look, and look! One of my first mentors as a teacher was Ben Doyle, who resides in Carmel, California. Ben was always saying, "Look, look, and look!" During the action phase of building a motion, your juniors need to use every sense they can. Obviously, taste, smell, and sound (auditory feedback is awesome if you can find it) will not do them too much good. So day in and day out they are left with two senses: sight and feel. For children, more times than not, they will stop looking and embrace the feel without verifying where the club actually is during the drill. This is a bad habit and a bad idea.

A simple fact is that the more you do something, the harder it is to feel. As children's muscles, tendons, ligaments, and skeleton move in a certain way, their feel will change. This development is normal. But, you must keep your junior golfer looking. They must take the time to understand how the movement feels. Take the time necessary to relate the movement to something they have done before. Take the time to describe how the movement feels. During the action phase of deliberate practice, the only things that will not change are the drill and having the player look and feel. After all, golf swings, as with all programs of movement, are built at a cellular level. Therefore, the length and tension relationship between muscles will change through movement.

This aspect of deliberate practice is so important for the youngster to understand because this aspect is where they will build (or solidify) their motions for the rest of their lives. Most juniors stop improving because they never understood highly refined practice and the complexities that come with it. Deliberate practice is not rocket science, but you should do it daily and you must look, look, and look!

Proper Reinforcement.

Let's turn our attention to reinforcement. When kids come in for a lesson, they just light up when they see how their swings have changed. It is hard for them to believe that all that swinging in front of the mirror has changed their motion so much. But look closely at what we are doing: We are placing the primary attention on their swings, not on ball flight. Some will say, "Hey! Paying attention to swinging is great. But all that matters is where the ball is going." I agree—if you are playing in a tournament. It is important to remember your child is wielding the club and inputting all the data into the ball. The ball responds to the delivery of the club. So what is more important: the swing or the ball flight? Does the club react to the swing? Yes. Does the ball react to the club? Yes.

There is no doubt that the motion is more important than the resulting ball flight. What you must teach your children is to re-enforce their process of deliberate practice rather than where the ball flies. When the golfer succeeds through the process of deliberate practice, the ball will start going where they want it to go. We must always reinforce the process. We must not reinforce the outcome. Giving way to sloppy practice habits and then scolding your child after a bad round is not sound thinking. I know that I am in the business of helping people with their outcome. But to help people with their outcome, I almost always have to fix their process.

The 70/30 Rule.

The instructor, i.e., me, only accounts for thirty percent of your child's success. I simply cannot reinforce everything your child learns from me. You the parent, and the process you create, grow, and emphasize account for the other seventy percent. Steering your child away from outcome and into the process is truly a team approach. The instructor needs to be a professional and give the correct information. The child needs to understand the motions and how often they should be done. The parent needs to reinforce the importance of the process during practice (and what practice really is). When we are learning new motions, we must not focus on the outcome.

If the process is correct, advancement becomes very simple. The child wants to get better. They are taken to an instructor. The instructor says do this drill six hundred times and come back. The child goes home and the parent holds them accountable for doing it thirty times daily for twenty days. If the outcome is not better, then the instructor might need to be replaced. Pretty simple, wouldn't you say?

But let me throw a little wrench into this cycle. You must remember that it is the brain that learns the new pattern, not the muscle. Standing somewhere and repeating a motion mindlessly is not the same as practicing with intention.

Practicing with Intention.

There are two basic ways to practice with intention. These two ways are called randomized practice and block practice. A deliberate golfer engages in **randomized practice** when he or she randomizes the task at hand. A deliberate golfer engages in **block practice** when attempting an exact task repeatedly. In study after study, you should know that **randomized intention** leads to greater retention than **block intention.**

A simple math example shows the difference between these two ways. Note that in both cases, the goal is to add two numbers together.

- This series of questions illustrates block practice: What is 213 + 33? What is 213 + 33? What is 213 + 33? What is 213 + 33? By the second time you read the question, you probably didn't have to think. You probably just answered the third question. By the fourth time you read the question, you might have been wondering, "What in the world am I reading?"

- This series of questions is an example of random practice: What is 234 + 14? What is 312 + 41? What is 563 + 11? This series of questions make you think, don't they?

Deliberate practice should make your child think by using random practice. So, you must look for intention as well as motion.

The reality is that your mind controls your muscles. This fact means that to build a motion, the repetitions must be done through block practice. When a junior golfer does nothing more than repeat the same motion over and over, however, they will overstate their confidence level. Then when thrown into a game full of variables (golf) they will fail. Therefore, on the driving range, the junior golfer must practice in a more random manner. That is, putting with one ball as they go through their normal putting routine. Or, when striking the ball, the junior changes clubs and targets from shot to shot while going through their normal full swing routine.

Watching some of the best players practice over the years has shown me that when players are really engaged (deliberate) in the drill, they will most likely randomize the motion. In other words, they will do the drill with a club, without a club, and possibly with different clubs. Their bodies will be integrating the "feel" as their minds are thinking about hitting certain shots. An important lesson is that the mind is extremely engaged during deliberate practice.

There are important caveats for practice sessions. As boredom, fatigue, or frustration set in, the performance will change. Boredom generally sets in because the session is lacking intention and deliberation. Fatigue generally sets in because the practice session is not defined. Frustration generally sets in because the feedback isn't provided effectively.

While boredom and fatigue are really self explanatory, proper feedback is not. Feedback should **not** be done as frequent, immediate, and informatively as possible. It is really a myth that we will perform better with constant, immediate feedback. The reason I am pointing this out is so that you are not the parent standing behind the child giving feedback constantly. Be patient on the range (or course) and let the child learn. Look for your chances to give feedback effectively.

If the practice process is incorrectly implemented, things become complicated. The child wants to get better. The instructor gives them a tip or two. The child goes to the range and the tip immediately feels uncomfortable. The ball flies sideways. The parent sees the outcome of the shot. The parent calls other folks to verify if the instructor is, in fact, a good one. After this investigation, the parent concludes that the instructor is a good one. Without reinforcement from the parent, the child starts to go back to what is comfortable. The parent, emotionally attached to outcome, thinks that as long as the outcome is fine, everything else must be fine. Maybe the golf gods will somehow get that club in a better place at the top. Who knows? The child is happy. Golf, however, remains a mystery. Notice that there is no accountability on the instructor, the child, or the parent. How can one expect improvement?

Here is an example of doing the practice process correctly. The child does the repetitions daily. When doing the repetitions, the child's mind is involved. The child is looking, using different clubs, and using imagery while making the motion. The motion is doing two things: building the motor pattern and providing the "feel." At the course, the child would be doing one of two things: building the pattern without concern of ball flight or testing the feel while going through their routines. The child takes the information from the tests and goes back to the deliberate practice for more acquisition of the skill. Notice that the outcome is ignored. In this example, improvement is highly likely.

But, eventually outcome does matter. Let's see where by talking about testing and tests. Testing is performance based to see what the player has retained through deliberate practice. Therefore, testing cannot be called practice in any sense. Examples of tests are making ten three foot putts in a row, hitting a high draw and then a high fade, tournaments, or any number of other events where a player is "testing" their feel. As you can imagine, the number of tests is practically limitless. The main lesson is to understand that testing is not practice. Practice focuses on building feel and repeatable patterns. Testing measures how much of these focus areas are retained.

Deliberate Practice, Reinforcement, and Confidence.

Let's return our focus to deliberate practice. Here are some specific examples:

- In front of a mirror, practice the correct ball position with a ball and alignment sticks.
- Stand on a wobble board and make putting strokes.
- Standing in front of a mirror adjusting the top of the swing to a more neutral position (while looking at the position, of course!)
- Sit on the couch and work on the grip by putting the club in the hands properly, waggling it, and then do it again.

Deliberate Practice comes in all shapes and forms, as you can see. Deliberate practice is done for a set amount of time or repetitions and the player is actively trying to accomplish the task at hand.

Let us examine the role of reinforcement in the deliberate practice context. Suppose a player is trying to adjust his motion while being emotionally attached to the outcome of the shot. This attachment makes improvement difficult to accomplish for both the player and the instructor. Even for the best players and instructor duos, practicing while having outcome attachment is difficult. When standing behind a tour player, instructors can assess swing issues easily.

When we start heading down the road of building swing thoughts and feelings we, as a team, must be extremely careful. The difference between tour players and your junior golfer is vast. Many tour players already have built their motion at a cellular level—with little compensation. The tour player has a subconscious skill set filled with talent. Your child, however, is building his motion and building his skill set.

I once had a very interesting conversation with a multiple winner on the tour about a leading sport psychologist. The tour player commented that, early in his career, he focused a lot on physical cues in his routine—like looks, and waggles. Over the years, the sport psychologist figured out if the best players in the world commit to the shot each time, their routines were the same.

So for the player and his psychologist, there was a shift in focus. Physical cues became less important than getting "committed" to the upcoming shot.

This sport psychologist has written many books and helped thousands of golfers on every level. If you picked up one of his books now, you would see less emphasis on physical routines and more emphasis on getting involved in the target. When information is disseminated across a broad range of different skill levels, some information will be targeted to a small specific group and some information will be targeted to a larger groups.

I think that every junior golfer could improve his sport specific movements during the swing. I also think that junior golfers naturally have a hero or icon. They want to act, practice, walk and talk like these people. They want their golf ball to fly like the golf ball of their hero. The danger of this way of thinking, however, is that junior golfers might put too much emphasis on ball flight. Consequently, practice becomes very sloppy. The same can happen if score is the focus. You, the parent, might think: "Tiger shot thirty-nine at age seven and so did Johnny today." This focus is dangerous. If one overlooks fundamental movement skills, sport specific skills, and the intricacies of deliberate practice and focus instead on the outcome of score, your junior golfer simply will not become all they could be in the game of golf.

Remember: You, the parent, are 70% of the equation. If you judge your child based on something they can control, like deliberate practice, you will greatly influence the rate at which your child builds confidence. Think of it like this: **Confidence is skill acquisition.** With the emphasis of acquiring skills in an area your child can control (i.e., deliberate practice), confidence will come. Here is an example of building confidence using deliberate practice. Building connection (that is, upper arms against the chest) in the golf swing by practicing it twenty times nightly is completely in the hands of the child. The result will be that the child's swing is connected while hitting a seven iron over water to a tucked pin on a firm green. This accomplishment comes from a group of skills including connection and confidence. Both skills are a result of deliberate practice.

Deliberate Practice Focuses on One Skill at a Time.

Deliberate practice does not cluster skill acquisition. Deliberate practice focuses on a single skill. More examples of deliberate practice:

- Work on the grip ten times.
- Work on the set up ten times.
- Work on getting into the lead leg ten times.

Importantly, separate these areas if you do them every day. Or, just focus on one area every day. After a couple of weeks, your child will find it easier and easier to do what they are practicing and their confidence grows as they acquire the skill.

Clustering skill acquisition will defeat the child nearly every single time when they are first learning the game. What do I mean by clustering skill acquisition? Here is an example. Little Johnny stands on the range. After a couple of misses, an onlooker trying to be helpful might say, "Keep your head down." Little Johnny hits one good one, and then misses a few more. The onlooker adds: "You need to turn a little more." Immediately a bad shot occurs. The onlooker says: "No, no, not like that. Keep your knees flexed." A good shot results but it is also followed by three more poor shots. The onlooker states: "Get your back to the target now at the top of your swing." What is going on? In this example there are four skills being clustered all the while the ball flight is being reviewed.

Here is an example of deliberate practice with a focus on one skill. The parent might say, "Let's do a little work today. I want you to make some practice swings with a balanced finish." The first swing is a little shaky. The second one is a little better. The next one is close. "Keep going, Johnny, until I see five good swings in a row. Then you can hit a shot." After fifteen or so attempts, Johnny gets five in a row nailed perfectly. The parent might add: "Hit a shot and hold the finish until the ball stops rolling." Little Johnny tops the ball, but he holds the finish until the ball stops rolling. The parent exudes: "Great job kiddo! Let's see five more perfect finishes!" What is going on here? One skill set with the child being rewarded. Note that the reward is not for the outcome (which he can't control), but for the motion (which is under his control).

It is obvious which example above will have little Johnny leaving the driving range with confidence. The sad part is many of you who represent the seventy percent of the equation, do not follow this type of deliberate practice and behavioral therapy. Instead, you often get involved in the ball flight, get emotionally sabotaged with the outcome, and try to fix the outcome. Please be careful. Make certain that you are helping your child acquire skills. Make sure you are leading them through the action phase of practice properly. Make sure you are reinforcing something that they can control (motion). Strive not to reinforce something they cannot control (ball flight).

Deliberate Practice and Noise.

In truth, golf is a game of variables. These variables are what make golf so difficult. The wind often changes during the round. The pin locations change daily. The putting surface changes throughout the day. For skill acquisition (aka confidence) to grow the instructor, the practice, and the parent cannot be variables. Instead, they must focus on what is desired during a session of practice and must make certain what is desired is something the child can control. Clustering skills (variables) and judging ball flight (variable) while judging the shot as good or bad as a parent (variable) is a recipe for frustration.

Deliberate practice is more than just mirror work or drills—it is where your mind is, too! Here are some examples. Playing golf with your friends where score is not kept versus playing golf with your friends with a medal on the line. Your son stands on the range hitting at a target an unknown distance away versus hitting at a target 98 yards away. Standing on the range hitting balls while you think your ball position is good versus hitting balls with sticks lying down giving you your ball position.

You see, deliberate practice is not what you are doing; it is how you are doing it. The simple reason is feedback. For your son or daughter to get better, they must get proper feedback. The scary thing, and possibly the most difficult concept, is trying to keep the "noise" out of the feedback. To me, "noise" is a way to describe the lack of learning that can take place during a practice session. Often, parents identify the enemy of their child's success is that their child talks and laughs with their friends while hitting ball after ball on the range. I believe "noise" goes much deeper than this jocularity.

"Noise" can come from the mind, the body, the parent, the coach, or any other variable when the intent of practice is not defined. As we saw earlier in this chapter, the parents that stand behind their child chiming off ten different thoughts are obviously noise. A body that is having trouble moving because of a growth spurt or dysfunction is noise. A coach that is constantly changing the message is noise. A mind that is not concentrated on the task at hand can create noise.

Deliberate Practice Has Intent.

A cornerstone to practice, deliberate practice at least, is to have the intent to accomplish a specific task during the session. This intent might be to figure out, and then practice, hitting high bunker shots. The intent could be on learning to punch out from the trees with a six iron. The intent might be on a weight shift or a steady head. **There must be intent.** There must also be the awareness that the junior golfer easily loses intent. Strange as it may sound, practicing for three minutes with intent is far better than practicing for 15 without intent.

Children can learn, unfortunately, to practice with "noise" all the time. They just hit the ball, hear a voice, make an assumption, change something, and then hit another ball. This cycle can be repeated and repeated without any intent. Then, when they enter a tournament, the "noise" really turns on. Dad is watching. The scorecard is in the back pocket. Everyone will be looking at the scores. Kids are everywhere hitting all kinds of shots. Remember, if these children have not really worked on anything deliberately, their scores change dramatically for the worse during tournament play. **There is so much "noise," the children cannot get feedback on what their job is that day of practice or in that tournament.**

This lack of feedback or "noise" bleeds its way through the anticipation phase of practice. It appears in the action phase when the child not being intent. It also forms a cloud over the reinforcement phase. "My child just doesn't have it," parents will say. "He just can't control his emotions on the course." Actually, your child is probably not being intent in his practice. Your child is most likely a bit confused on what they should actually be doing during practice. You see, there is nothing wrong with your child—the process that he is practicing is wrong. Again: Nothing is wrong with your child—it is the fact that they are practicing the wrong kind of "practice."

Clustering Tasks Creates a Lot of Noise.

Deliberate practice eliminates as much "noise" as possible. Your child is deliberately practicing when they are regularly practicing with intent and focusing on one area he needs to fix. This area could be mental, physical, or technical. If there is more than one focus in these areas, I recommend that they not be mixed or clustered. In other words, if your child is working on his routine, do not worry about the swing. If your child is working on her technique, do not worry about where the ball flies. If your child is working on physical skill, leave the swing reminders out.

When a player is simultaneously working on ball flight, technique, and routine there is simply too much noise. When a player is on the course working on their swing while judging their score, there is too much noise. This type of task clustering makes it nearly impossible to practice with intent. Sounds simple doesn't it? I would suspect, however, clustering tasks is where parents make their most dreadful decisions and, therefore, their biggest mistakes.

Parents must help their children focus on a single task. For example, this task might be a specific type of bunker shot. Obviously, the club face must be open and the club path will be a bit outside to inside. First, have your youngster set up with an open face and make swings outside to in. Then, draw a line in the sand and have them make the same motion, with the same face, and hit the spot they are looking at. Note that a ball has not been hit yet. Ask them to do this drill twenty times each day. After they have made their twenty motions, bring the ball into the equation. If all is good, then hit some shots; however, as soon as difficulty begins, get rid of the ball. This is a great example of deliberate practice because the process has intent. The intent is to acquire and master the ability of swinging the club out to in with an open face and hit the sand where the child wishes. Simply hitting bunker shots is not deliberate, because intention is lost when the focus is on ball flight.

Your child should do this for two to three weeks for a certain amount of time each day during practice. Follow a schedule of practice. I assure you that PGA Tour players do not have to do this each practice session because they are already experts at it. Look closely at the practice sessions on Tour and you will see "mini sessions" of these intentional motions all the time. As your child progresses, you can create another deliberate practice session after three weeks or so. Maybe the focus will be on an even more open face or possibly the task is to work on the routine in the bunker. Whatever the case, always define the intention of the practice for your child. Remember: **At first, keep the ball out of the equation and put attention on the process**.

The Path to Excellence.

I hope that you are now thinking that the path to excellence requires hours of intentional effort. It does. Remember: **Practice must be something that your child can control and must be intentional.** Dumping out a pile of range balls and hitting at a target is not practice. Taking your child to the range and expecting them to think about their golf swing while you judge their ball flight is not practice. These "practice" attempts are far too noisy! On the other hand, having your child practice a simple task such as ball position for ten minutes and then taking them on the course and having them intentionally run their mental routines is practice. Again **confidence is skill acquisition**, because a child can work on ball position and then they can run their routines on the course. When we throw in ball flight, score, and doing so with a perfect ball position as they run their routine, the practice gets entirely too noisy. When practice gets noisy, learning will grind to a halt because clustering multiple tasks becomes too much for the child (or adult) to handle.

Nearly every week, I give a lesson to someone who believes he can think his way through the golf swing. You probably experience the same type people in everyday life, those that just keep adding and adding until you can almost hear the "noise." **Becoming proficient, or elite, at a movement is really**

a result of electrical impulses carried through about 100 billion "wires" between our ears. They are basically God's wiring, with neurons being connected together through synapses. So the bunker shot, the chip shot, or simply the grip are by-products of a fancy light show going on at a cellular level.

Muscle Memory really doesn't exist. Simply stated, the more we use a motion, the more the electrical impulses fires until the circuitry is built at a cellular level. This circuitry development at a cellular level is then seen or felt as being second nature; hence the concept of muscle memory. This area is a tricky one, because those players that have created "great circuitry" will often tell you they have always possessed the skill. It is a grand illusion. I have never seen a child hold a club for the first time and then swing it with competence.

Physiology and Deliberate Practice.

"Have you ever stopped to think that movement is as much of a biological imperative as food and water? It is. There was a time, and not long ago, when it was easy, instinctive, to obey the biological imperative of motion." ---Pete Egoscue

So we grab a ball and toss it in the air. We toss it again. We toss it again. What is happening? The neurons and synapses fire (electrical impulses) to make the motion, other cellular bodies, oligodendrocytes sense the commotion and gets in the middle of the party. These cells, the oligodendrocytes, then begin to wrap and squeeze on the electrical impulse finally leaving behind a sheath like structure called myelin. **Myelin is what transforms a movement from a "dial-up connection" to a "broadband connection."**

Deliberate practice fires the electrical impulses again, and again, and again. The whole time, at a cellular level, another event is taking place as the oligodendrocytes are getting in the mix. These cells are grasping, wrapping and spinning around the impulse thereby insulating and speeding it up. So skill acquisition happens at a cellular level. This is why skill acquisition takes time. The exact amount of time cannot be readily estimated because our brains seemingly get different amounts of myelin at different times.

Eventually the deliberate practice of throwing the ball into the air has created a cellular change. The electrical impulse from the neuron to the synapse has been encased in a sleek pathway, thanks to myelin. Finally throwing the ball into the air is quite simple or even second nature. As you can see, it is not the cognitive thought that creates this skill; it is the reaction of movement at a cellular level.

This cellular activity reacts to movement. You cannot think your way to this cellular reaction. You cannot think your way to elite movement. The firing of the circuitry must take place time and time and time again. It requires action. It requires a mind. Building cellular reaction is why movement in multiple planes is so important. Building cellular reaction is why practicing intently or deliberately is so important. Because cellular change takes place over time, the establishment of a designed practice regiment is the pathway to acquiring cellular reaction.

It is also apparent that age matters. It appears that myelin is more prominent in stages or waves. The variables are not completely known but two of them are DNA and activity. An early start, or at least a timely start, can be crucial. As we all know, being at the right place at the right time can make all the difference. It appears this same concept applies on a cellular level as well. Getting the right movements, in the right context, at the right times is very important.

Research supports the idea that elite performance happens at a cellular level. It is not a child winning and then gaining the confidence to continue to win that creates a great golfer. On the contrary, is the firing of the neurons and the deliberate practice that gives the child a winning movement pattern.

A Short Final Thought.

Please do not get the cart before the horse. Do not seek a win to applaud. Instead, insist on steady, deliberate practice and let the chips fall where they may. Applaud the practice and understand the process is slow, steady, and difficult. Failure, after all, is the backbone of success. The road to mediocrity is smooth. The road to elite performance is strenuous, long, and as rough as the surface of the moon.

Practice can be playing golf and working on your routine. Practice can be learning to read different lies around the green. Practice can be in front of a mirror doing a drill. Playing four holes and really concentrating on a particular task each day is much better than playing 54 holes on Saturday. Keep it simple, keep it intentional, keep it steady, and, above all, keep your focus on the process—not the outcome.

Chapter Lessons:

- Avoid thinking during your swing. Thinking while hitting does not work. Teach yourself to hit the ball with an empty mind.
- Driving ranges, by design, are profit centers (or fun centers)
- Practice should be specifically designed to improve performance.
- Monitor the practice habits of your children, not the outcomes of their swings.
- Random practice and Block practice are different.
- Seventy percent of the solution occurs away from your teaching professional.
- Deliberate practice requires deliberate mental attention.
- Deliberate practice will calm down "the noise."
- Your child should be in control of their own practice—they should practice on what they can control.
- Give your child practice tasks that they can accomplish. Confidence stems from acquiring skills. Deliberate practice changes movement and engrains patterns at a cellular level.
- You must test your skills periodically. But, make sure you realize that testing is not practice.

Our Inner Dummies

Introduction.

Why do golfers choke? Why does a young junior golfer shoot even par in a practice round and then play worse during the tournament? How can I help my child stay in check emotionally and just play golf? This chapter introduces some key terms of the mental game: The Limbic Brain, Emotional Sabotage, Routine, Inner Dummy, and The Path to Anxiety. This chapter will arm you with the understanding of what is happening in the brain of your child. It will give you areas to focus on when you are talking to them about preparation for a tournament.

We often hear about making each day special or that we should be living for the moment. The truth is that most days are spent in the same basic model. Each evening we are in some type of **rest/relax period** in which we watch a little television, visit with our family, and get some sleep. During this period we generally begin to **assimilate a plan** for the following day. Upon waking, we begin to implement our plan. Sure, we brush our teeth and shower. We might even listen to music or a podcast as we commute--but there is a **plan**.

Not too long into our day we will be hit by a **stimulus**. This **stimulus** is perceived as either negative or positive as it fits into our **plan** for the day. Once the stimulus hits, we gets emotional. "Yes! This is exactly what I thought would happen!" Or, "There is no way this could happen right now! C'mon, man!"

Commonly, one of two things happen: we either revert to our **routine** or we become **emotionally hijacked**. Businesses have procedures built in to sales or customer service so that when stimulus hits, the employee will have a routine to follow. These procedures keep the employee and customer from being emotionally sabotaged or hijacked.

This cycle of **rest/relax, plan, implementation of plan, stimulus, routine/or emotional hijacking happens each day.** So what does this have to do with junior golf? Well, it is quite simple. Young Johnny is lying down for bed. He has played his practice round and is going over a few of the shots he will need to hit tomorrow. A few minutes later, he is asleep. Morning comes and it is now time to get ready. The plan starts. On number three, a stimulus hits with a missed seven iron and a three putt. Double bogey! Is Young Johnny going to be emotionally hijacked?

More importantly let's look at Old Johnny, Young Johnny's dad. Old Johnny drove his son three hours across the state line for this tournament. He walked around with him during the practice round to provide support for his son.

At dinner, they talked about the tournament and created a plan. (Most likely Old Johnny provided much of the plan.) On the way to the course, Old Johnny went over a few more strategic tips. The missed seven iron was not part of the plan. "Two over through three holes," Old Johnny thinks to himself.

The round continues. Old Johnny stays with it emotionally until the eighth hole when a three-putt bogey gets Young Johnny to three over for the tourney. "I am a whole state away from home and this rascal has already blown his chance to win. He has completely out of it before making the turn. Maybe he can birdie the ninth hole and get it back!"

On the ninth hole, Young Johnny hits a less than perfect tee shot that carries the fairway bunker, hits the cart path and bounds over the white stakes. Old Johnny drops his head. "You have to be kidding me! Come on son! We went over this yesterday!" he says to himself. Young Johnny feels humiliated, let down, and knows what his father is thinking.

Now, do you think these two are **emotionally hijacked?** Have you been there? I think we have all been there either as players or parents. This type of behavior is obviously tied to outcome much more than process. The stimulus of the score has emotionally hijacked the pair. When they will get back to routine is not known. It might be on the tenth hole, at dinner, or next week after they get back to the normal daily cycles. But where does this type of behavior come from?

It comes from the brain. More specifically it comes from the sub neo-cortex. This area of our brain drives, holds, and controls emotional impulses that surge over us like waves. For our purposes, we will call this system the limbic system. This system is different from our rational system. The emotional brain and the rational brain are always competing. The problem with the limbic system, and its drive of the emotional brain, is that it seems to fight rational thinking. Think of the example of Old Johnny and Young Johnny: Why can't they see that it is only a golf tournament? Why are they living and dying with every shot out there? The reason is because their limbic systems are in control.

Core Limbic Drives.

There are five core limbic drives. We will start with **sexual drive**. The old saying, "More great players have been lost to perfume, alcohol, and gasoline than anything else!" speaks to the power of the limbic drive. Sexual attraction is very easy to identify with and it is exceedingly easy to see those hormones kick in and change our children's actions and behaviors.

Next is our **power drive.** It is the pecking order isn't it? It is the reason we don't like people that always seem to beat us. It is the reason we still get that uneasy feeling when someone blows it by us thirty yards off the tee. Taken to excess, it is the source of envy, jealousy, or hatred.

Another drive is our **survival drive.** We must live to fight another day. Right? This drive is also the area where many irrational fears or anxieties surface. Have you ever felt like your son or daughter "had" to get the ball in the fairway? If so you have experienced the survival drive.

Next is the **territorial drive.** Have you ever gotten angry when someone hit your new club? Have you ever felt like it was more difficult or possibly easier to win at your home course? This was, or is, part of the enigmatic story of Mr. Hogan in 1953 when he went to The Open Championship for the first time and won!

Finally, there is a drive that underlies the reason why I am writing this book, **nurturance.** It is hard to say that that any of us would deem this drive as undesirable. This drive is the reason we like to form attachments to others, to build relationships, and to be a part of the "herd."

This limbic system is really a group of structures in the brain that are associated with emotions. It is not a stand-alone part of our brain—it is also associated with behavior learning, smell, and long-term memory. That is, you should not get the idea that the limbic system is some grapefruit sized tumor generating evil.

Over the years, rats and other animals have been put through experiments that manipulated the limbic system's four main structures: the amygdala, the hippocampus, the limbic cortex and the septal area. The results are sometimes darkly humorous and remind me of the way teenagers and parents can act. My favorite experiment was published in 1954. Two researchers (Olds and Milner) placed electrodes into areas of the limbic system on rats. Each time the rat pressed on a certain lever, the researchers would stimulate the rat's limbic system. The rats went on to ignore food or water. Eventually, the rats died from exhaustion from continuously pressing on the lever!

As it turns out, when areas of the limbic system have been taken out of animals they become tame. Often times, they lose the motivation to eat or drink. So if your teenager will not calm down, understand there is a radical cure: Remove parts of the limbic system! All kidding aside, you, the parent, must understand that your child's brain is not so much different than your own. No two brains are the same (thank heavens) but your child and you will always be emotional creatures. In fact, it is this limbic system of drives that can be either harnessed (and helpful) or unfettered (and harmful).

So, let's go back to the example of Young Johnny. When he completes the round, his score is 80! While he is obviously emotionally upset, he searches for something to default to so that he can quiet down the limbic system. Old Johnny has been emotionally sabotaged for going on three hours now. He also senses a need for some emotional tranquility. So what do they do?

Should Young Johnny go hit balls? Should Old Johnny go hit the bar? Should Young Johnny go get something to eat and rest? Should Old Johnny kick in the power drive and jumped down his son's throat? **Emotional Sabotage is so difficult because anxiety is floating everywhere at golf tournaments!**

Both Young and Old Johnny will return to rest and relax. They will both formulate a different plan. They will both implement the plan and a stimulus will appear. When it does, the limbic system will kick in once more. The sad part, however, is two-fold. First, if the outcome, i.e., winning the tournament, is the primary focus, neither Johnny can avoid being emotionally sabotaged. Second, they both will see "emotion" as the problem and will probably waste considerable mental energy trying to "feel" positive.

To provide a new look at this situation, let's start with the central theme of this book. **Placing your emphasis on winning is not only wrong—it's disastrous.** Golf is a game of variables. Each hole is different, each putt is different in length and break, each day the wind is different. The list can go on and on. One thing, however, is certain: The variables are what make the game difficult. If every hole in golf looked the same and the conditions were always the same, golf would be (relatively) easy. If you want to experience considerable failure at the sport of golf, teach your children (or yourself) to be an additional variable in this game of variables.

So how do you, the parent, protect yourself from being emotionally sabotaged without resorting to chemicals (i.e., a prescription of Zanex)? The way to protect yourself begins by placing your emphasis on routine, not on outcome. Why do you think business managers have protocol for dealing with different items of business? It is their routine. By going back to the learned and practiced routine of handling difficult stimuli, the employees and managers can get through the variables of day to day business.

Mental Toughness.

Similarly, your junior golfer can get through the variables the game presents if they have a protocol. In golf, we call protocol "our routine." Therefore, if you place your emphasis on having your child going through their routine on each shot, you are giving your child a chance to minimize the impact of the variables the game presents. If you want to avoid emotional sabotage, place your focus on routine.

I think of "mental toughness" as being "mentally defined." Golfers on the path to success know what they can control on the golf course. Parents who have placed their child on the path to success also know what their child can control on the golf course. That is, both the child and the parent know that the only thing they can control is getting committed to the shot and hitting it with the same physical and mental protocol each time.

Defining your physical and mental protocol is a major topic in sports psychology. Emotional sabotage will not occur if the only goal of each shot on each hole during each round is to run through a mental and physical routine. The routine is specific, constant, and the child has control of their routine. Will your child still get angry over the results of a shot? Sure. Any competitor will. Will you still get let down by the results of a shot, a hole, or a round? Sure, what parent wouldn't? The backbone of success is failure. The key is to channel anger at failure into an even more dedicated focus on routine.

I suspect, however, that many of you believe that having a great routine will lead to lower scores and better shots immediately. Sadly, this belief is simply not true. Defining the routines used in the full swing, short game, and putting is the first step. Practicing these routines is the second step. Successfully integrating these routines during tournament play is the third step. Along the way, you will still see bad shots and scores that upset you, but your child is on the path to minimizing possible errors.

You must realize that improvement in this game comes through a process of elimination. By defining a routine and defining the child's primary focus on the course, the mind will not be the reason for poor performance. Therefore, for me at least, the greatest power of the physical and mental routine on the course is ruling out the mind as the source of any mistakes that occur. Golf swings and bodies can be fixed as long as the mind is a constant. I really have no answers for players whose minds are a variable. In these cases, players are easy targets for emotional hijackings. My experience tells me an emotionally hijacked player cannot be fixed.

Initially, understand the physical and mental routines are the key to eliminating mental mistakes on the course. By signaling the routine the same way each time and having the same number of looks (each one should have a purpose) the player will be choosing to be a constant in a game of variables. **Once the routine has been practiced and has become the primary focus, there will be much less emotional sabotaged for players and the parents of players.**

The parent will be able to memorize the routine and know when something changes. All you can ask of your children is to prepare correctly and then go out and run their routine on each shot. If their golf swing does not perform, they will still miss shots. If their bodies are dysfunctional, they will still miss shots. If their strategy is incorrect, they will still miss shots. If their green reading skills are poor, they will still miss putts. Thankfully, however, golf swings, bodies, strategies, and green reading skill can all be fixed in the presence of a routine. Asking your child to concentrate on a routine is giving them a task that they can control. Asking (or expecting) them to win this tournament or that tournament is simple insanity that almost always leads to emotional disasters.

Science tells us this about emotion: Emotion sharpens our skills to a point, but when too much emotion appears, our skills cannot be used. **Attempting to mitigate emotion on the course is wasted effort.** If there is too much emotion, the process is not the primary focus. By keeping the focus on performing the physical and mental routine, emotions will be kept in check. However, I see so many parents that say, "My son/daughter just doesn't have it up here!" Hogwash! These parents are ones who believe that the level of mental skills cannot grow. **The truth is that when emotions run too high, the outcome has become the primary focus.**

Reflect and ask yourself: When do you get anxious on the golf course? Anxiety in and of itself is not the problem. Emotions themselves are not the problem. Anxiety and emotion are symptoms of the primary focus being on the outcome of the shot. The limbic system cannot be turned off and on. If the primary goal is something attainable on each shot, then emotions will not run too high. If the primary goal is something that might be attainable based on some outcome-oriented measure, then emotions will run too high.

I will return to emotions in a moment but let me first give you an example. When I was a kid my father would come out and time my routine. In truth, we didn't really know what a routine did; we just knew that routines were in all the golf magazines. We came up with 22 seconds as the time of my routine. The only problem was that I loved playing golf with the men's group at our club. A 22-second routine stuck out like a sore thumb amongst a bunch of guys that played eighteen holes in three hours. So as soon as my father caught me not going through my 22-second routine, he became emotionally hijacked. I was probably 12 or 13 but I remember the lecture he gave me riding from the sixth green to the seventh tee. The choices boiled down to either go play by myself and run my 22-second routine, or continue to play with the guys and deep six the routine. Of course, I chose the men's group.

But you see my father and I had it wrong. A routine does not take 22 seconds. In fact, adding stuff to a routine just to add it is the opposite of why we have a routine. The goal is to get the conscious mind involved a step-by-step process that allows the sub-conscious skill of the player to appear repeatedly. The goal is for the step-by-step process to be the primary focus so the limbic system doesn't kick in and turn our perfectly functioning driving range swing into a collection of lurches on the golf course.

Routines and Pre Shot Routines.

Look at it this way. Suppose concentrating on the target is our true goal. Therefore, we need a routine to achieve this goal. So, running our routine is now our goal. The goal of concentrating on the target can be viewed as a by-product of running the routine. When a player is really just playing golf and concentrating on the target, they will do the same thing each time. Think of what happens, however, to that same player when more variables are added (like a tournament, trophies, stature in the club, adulation of peers, etc.). Adding these variables to the outcome will likely lead the player to perceive that the shot is more than just a shot. Now if the routine is not defined, then what does the player make as the primary focus of the shot? The routine or the outcome? Most likely, it is the outcome—which has a negative effect of the actual outcome. By making routine the primary focus, however, the player maximizes the likelihood of a good outcome.

A typical routine starts with a physical signal. The signal might be tugging on the shirt or putting both hands on the club in the full swing. The routine might proceed by looking at the target for alignment as you set up to the ball. From there, the routine continues with a confirmation look at the target and proceed to swing. In this example, the routine is quite simple and fast (8 to 13 seconds on average):

- Physical signal
- 1st look for alignment
- 2nd look to confirm the target
- Go!

By contrast, my father and I were building an elaborate routine that involved practice swings, strategy, breaths, looks, etc. Our mistake was very common: **We thought a good routine had to be an elaborate routine.** Building a routine will take more than an hour probably, but not much. Just video your child on the course and ask them why they are doing what they are doing. Define why they are looking at the target. Define the physical signal at the beginning of the routine. Then, make a video your child going through the newly defined routine. Talk about how concentrating on this routine results in the best shot given the variables that they cannot control.

Pre-shot routines are different from the routine that we have been discussing. Pre-shot routines involve strategy, practice swings, and decision making. These practice swings and decisions are not part of your routine because a pre-shot routine is not constant—it can be unique to each shot. For example, if I am faced with an easy chip shot, I might not even take a practice swing. If my ball is buried four inches deep in Bermuda grass, however, I might need to take five practice swings to get committed to the shot. The point is that you must understand that a pre-shot routine and the routine are different.

My guess is that most people do not understand this distinction. They think that playing golf with a routine slows them down. Quite the opposite is true. As a general rule, people take ages over the golf ball before they swing. They make a decision on the club (or the line of the putt) rather quickly, then they walk up to the ball, and turn on their minds! This process is the opposite of a routine. Figure out the shot and rehearse your swing if you want. When you are committed to the shot, think of nothing but your routine. For example: physical signal, first look for alignment, second look to confirm target, and go! Do you see the difference between a typical process and what is a constant routine?

Choking.

I really do not think choking exists. Of course, we have all felt our brains switch gears. We have all felt (note feeling is an emotion) when this shot or this putt was really important. What do we perceive? We perceive the outcome. We perceive that if this crucial putt falls, we will be closer to our desired outcome. Do you see how the outcome is now your focus? If the outcome becomes your primary focus, your limbic system sees its chance to "do its dance." A mixture of neurons, synapses, nerves, chemicals, and different areas of the brain ignite and a system as old as the human race kicks in. Now you are aware! The small appendages begin to shake as adrenaline kicks in. On the outside we look normal, but on the inside we are churning.

Does this sound like a recipe for choking? Well it is not. It is normal. Every great athlete will tell you (after they are retired) they went through this same set of events. They knew, however, that they were only in control of the process. They defaulted to the series of events that they could control. As you should be thinking by now, a focus on what you can control is a routine.

Simply stated, choking is really just being emotionally sabotaged. The inner dummy is fully on display for public viewing, and the limbic system is doing a sack dance over the poor outcome.

All golfers learning about the game of golf must understand how they can easily become emotionally sabotaged. The apparent way the brain and mind fight one another is the way we are all made. All those voices you hear over a putt? Limbic System. That feeling of total loss of motor control? Limbic System. It is your inner dummy struggling to escape because a stimulus has appeared. You are at the crossroads between becoming emotionally hijacked and regaining control. The road to regaining control is to make the running of your routine your primary focus.

Every young golfer will benefit greatly from a parent who is knowledgeable in the ways of a routine. A deep and unshakable belief in keeping the process the primary objective is necessary to attain your goals. Defaulting to the routine is a learned skill. The parent must "buck the system" if you will and grade the performance at the tournament by how well their entrant followed the routine throughout the tournament. That is, the score is secondary to the routine. When your children understands and buys into the notion that running the routine is the primary objective, "choking" will disappear.

What we now know, scientifically speaking of course, is the conscious mind becomes aware of emotions after the emotions have begun. Emotions literally take place before conscious awareness. This fact means that part of your child's brain (or yours) is beginning a process of appraisal that sets emotion in motion before the conscious mind has a chance. Note the words; "a process of appraisal." Our brains are constantly appraising situations on a sub-conscious level. Why do you think we sometimes wonder what our faces looked like after hearing or seeing a strange event?

I remember a young student of mine who went on to a superb college to play Division 1 golf. He was a state high school champion in golf and a state junior champion. He had good skills and understood the game. After a delightful first year it was time to take it to the next level. Enter sports psychologist. One spring day, he came up to do some work on his game and discuss his play. He wasn't getting much out of his game and, by all basic appearances, he was in a slump. The golf swing was in order. The ball flight was in order. The pitching and putting motion was in order. I was a bit perplexed so we decided to go out on the course.

Because I had known him since he was a youngster and because I had played several rounds with him, I had a feel for his pace of play. What I found on the course was a different player. He was standing behind the ball. Visualizing the shot I would assume. The routine was long, with practice swings and deep breaths. Out of curiosity, I asked him what he was doing during this seemingly endless period before hitting the ball. "Trying to wipe the slate clean," was his remark. I went on to identify this as meaning trying to get rid of any negative emotion before embarking on the shot.

Do you understand what he was doing? He was trying to get rid of emotions through his conscious, rational mind. He was trying to stop them. The only problem was they were forming before he even realized it. **Trying to become a machine that hits every shot with the perfect amount of emotion is not the aim of a routine.** Emotions will flare up on their own as your child gets closer or further from the goal. The goal of a routine is to run the routine and let the outcome take care of itself.

This type of thinking sets neatly on shelf along with deliberate practice and functional training. This type of thinking has little in common with ball beating and early specialization. Children are inherently smart. They know when they are pushing themselves to learn. They know when they are pushing their bodies to move better. It will be difficult for the child that does not practice with intention to then make a routine primary on the course. It will be very difficult for the aspiring college player, who has specialized in golf starting at age eleven, to make the process primary.

The limbic system has been called "the devil's playground." My father referred to it as the "mental midget." Whatever you wish to call the limbic system is fine. Sometimes I refer to it as "the genius" in a rather sarcastic tone. What you must understand is the limbic system is not your child. It is part of your child, just as it is part of you. It has been passed down through the generations of human civilization via DNA. Everyone from Jack Nicklaus to your child has battled his or her inner dummies. It happens on the baseball field, the soccer field, and in NASCAR.

Speaking of NASCAR, I recently had the opportunity to sit down with one of the most renowned sport psychologist of our era. He has worked with professional and collegiate players on a variety of levels and in a variety of sports. One of his best stories revolved around a NASCAR driver that came to him to improve his performance on the track.

"After a little conversation I asked him how I could help him," the doc said. "Well doc," the racer said, "I am not scared. Being scared won't get you past the dirt track circuit. But there is this one thing...."

"Go on." The doc said.

"Well at 185 mph this #3 car (Dale Earnhart) will get inches from my rear bumper. Then he will start tapping his index finger on the top of steering wheel motioning for me to get over or else. I am having a tough time getting that out of my mind."

Anxiety.

Why is it that golf seems to breed fear, anxiety, and, for a lack of better term, will make a player "play scared?" As a child we all played aggressive sports at one point or another. It might have been football, boxing, rugby, or ice hockey. We have all felt that turning of our stomachs and that rush of adrenaline. Every time I see a picture of Eddy Vedder stage diving into a sea of people I think of boxing. That is really what it felt like. Once the bell sounds to start the bout, you were in the air. Seconds later, you were out of breath and could feel the punches landing. I have heard a similar account when people talk about playing football. The anxiety leaves when the buzzer sounds.

But it is often not that way in golf. Often times our children and ourselves cannot shake the anxiety can we? Before you rule yourself or your children as people that don't have the mental make up to be a great champion, let's look at why this happens.

First there must be some sort of emotion creating *worry*. *Worrying* about score maybe, or maybe what other players will think of you. For *worry* to grow, there must be some sign that it could happen to you and there must be a substantial amount of time for you to find out if it will. We have all seen the expression on the faces of junior golfers as Roy (who made a nine on #7) recounts his adventure through bunkers, trees, deep grass, and finally into the hole. On the PGA Tour, when this type of talk starts up players will absolutely walk off. It is like a plague. Who wants to catch the plague?

With time for the *worry* to grow, all we need now are three simple mental steps. *1) Imagine yourself doing it.* Just take a second to see you topping it in the creek on #7. *2) Imagine yourself not doing that at all. In fact, fight the emotion by telling yourself it is impossible for that to happen to you.* This takes a little self-talk. You must fight the emotion with another emotional voice from your limbic system. *3) Try to figure out a way to avoid that shot.* Now we have *Anxiety!* Not only that, we have at least a couple of hours before we get to the 7th hole so there is plenty of time for it to really creep into our emotions.

Going back to *worry,* if the child's job is to run their routine and that is the primary objective, do you think there will be any emotion to grow? First remember, for *worry* to grow, there must be a sign that it could happen (seeing a good player hitting a bad shot or hearing Roy's account of his nine) and time for the worry to present itself. This type of worry is totally outcome oriented. If the child's primary aim is to run their physical/mental routine, the seeds of worry will be quickly bagged up mentally.

Secondly, for *anxiety* to set in, the child has to see himself making the mistake. They will do so, I assure you. All it takes for anxiety to emerge is a second of visualization. Then, your child must fight this visual with another visual. They will try the second visual also—but this process is wasted mental energy.

Fighting an emotion with another emotion is simply a losing proposition. You are much better off by ignoring the emotional voice. When routine is primary, the emotional voice can be bagged up. So finally, the child needs to figure out a way to prevent anxiety from happening. Anxiety appears in the form of stomach aches, complaints about tournament golf, and sudden injuries.

But don't you see that **worry turns to anxiety because the outcome is the primary objective.** Parents of these children that do not understand the process will often say to me, "VJ, I think I am going to let his mother caddy for him." Or it might come out as "VJ, my son/daughter just don't have the right wiring for this game. They are good at every sport but this game gets under their skin."

Step back and look at the picture clearly. The child has either not been taught a routine or has not practiced it enough. They are still clutching the "outcome" just as they did their favorite toy at age three. It is the parent's and coach's job to get into that child's mind and change their mind-set. I told you that you were 70% of the recipe didn't I? It is not that children don't have the mental aptitude for golf; it is they don't have the mental training for a sport consisting of so many subtle variables and one that takes so much time to practice and play.

The reason golf can put more fear into the mind's of golfers (like that #3 car could to another driver) stems from **time.** Look at this equation:

The Limbic System + Time + Fighting The Emotion + A Lack Of Proper Preparation + The Outcome Being Primary = An Inner Dummies Riot!

This is the true equation for those children that cannot get over the hump of competitive golf because they get emotionally hijacked on the course. The parents of these players can usually be spotted pacing the cart paths, biting their fingernails, and kicking trees. Living and dying with each shot, these parents are emotionally hijacked. Let's look at another equation.

The Limbic System + Time + Ignoring the voice of the emotion + Proper Preparation + The Routine Being Primary = A Champion's Mind.

This equation summarizes where the best hang out. They don't fight the emotion. They don't have some special inner being that is taking emotion and throwing it out the window of their biological body. They are simply concerned with doing their best, and their best is taking care of what they can take care of: getting in tune with the target and hitting the shot.

Chapter Lessons:

- **Understand the Daily Cycle**
- **The Limbic System has 5 basic Drives**
- **Emotional Sabotage will happen—just understand what it is and how to overcome it.**
- **The Mental/Physical Routine is the key to eliminating mental mistakes on the course. Your child may still make strategic, mechanical, or physical mistakes on the course.**
- **Floating Anxiety is a sign of being Emotionally Hijacked.**
- **Attempting to mitigate emotion on the course is a waste of mental energy.**
- **An elaborate routine may not be a good routine.**
- **Choking exist only when a person is emotionally sabotaged.**
- **Trying to hit shots with the perfect amount of emotion on each shot is not the aim of a routine.**
- **Worry turns into Anxiety because the outcome is the primary objective.**
- **Create an equation that gives your child the best chance of becoming great. Then, practice it.**

INSIGHTS

I conducted a series of interviews during the winter of 2011. Note that I have not revealed the identities of the people being interviewed. If you really have to know who this person is, there are plenty of tips given. So, if you do a little digging, you will be able to figure it out. *Her father's insights are in italicized text.*

I met this player in 2009. Initially she needed help putting and a direction to move toward with her full swing. In 2012, she will be a rookie on the LPGA Tour. Her story is just beginning.

"How many sports did you play growing up?"

"Golf, ice-skating, ballet, tap, jazz, gymnastics, softball, soccer, cheerleading, violin, choir, musical-theater, etc., I really did a lot."

"At age three, she was into tap, golf, ballet. At five, it was ballet, tap, soccer, and golf. At seven, it was ballet, tap, jazz, ice-skating, golf, gymnastics, and music-theater. At ten, it was ballet, tap, jazz, ice-skating, violin, golf, gymnastics, vocal lessons, softball, cheerleading, and precision skating. At thirteen, it was ballet, tap, jazz, ice skating, violin, golf, gymnastics and vocal lessons."

"When did you start playing golf?"

"I started swinging a club really young. I was swinging the club by age three. At five years old I started playing golf on real courses. I remember a huge nature preserve close to my house where we would go hit balls when I was a kid. There was also a par three course 30 minutes from the house we would go to. By six years old, I could play with my dad without interrupting him too much."

"She had a course laid out around the house when she was a child. You could hear her two blocks away when she made a birdie from all the hollering we would do. All the mulch around the tree was a sand trap. By six years old she could hit the ball with some authority.

"On a Sunday morning when she was seven or eight, we went to the first tee and there were the guys waiting in the background. One was grumbling about a dad and a little girl teeing off, it probably had something to do with slow play or something. She got up and ripped it right down the middle. You should have heard all his buddies start giving him grief for complaining."

"When did golf become the sport?

"By age 16 it was golf. Time had become an issue. A friend, Brittany Johnston and I would play some of the Future Tour World Collegian events during the school year. In the summers my mom, Laura, and I would be gone two weeks a month playing different events. I would play AJGA events and USGA qualifiers.

"It was hard for me when I was younger because I was so much different from them. There were no other kids that wanted to play the LPGA Tour at seven or eight years old. There were no girls to practice with. It is not very often that we have the opportunities to get it all right, so I had to do a lot of the practice on my own. I didn't mind doing it by myself. I didn't mind that there was nobody else that shared my passion when I was that young, but I do remember being out there a lot by myself."

"The whole philosophy, with our resources, was to expose the children to as many things as possible. A lot of our philosophy came from my wife. Laura has her masters in early childhood development. We felt like the key was the children needed to develop a passion for their talents. I knew in my heart from the first time I saw her swing a club there was something special there. When she was a child she would sit in front of the television all afternoon watching the pros play. There was something special there. We knew that we would nurture that but expose her to other things.

"We (her mom and I) were different because we worried about burnout in any activity. At the core of it was education—both intellectually and physically. Physical literacy was the whole reason we exposed them to so many things. A lot of that comes from my wife. She really believed in physical and mental literacy.

"She would get so serious so quick when it came to golf! At a young age, we always accentuated the positive for her. Our focus was on the fun. There were a lot of cheerleading and high fives going when she was hitting quality shots. It is easy to lose the fun when the seriousness started to percolate but we did all we could."

"It sounds like you were incredibly busy as a child. Can you elaborate on that time?"

"Yeah, we were. Mom would have home cooked dinners in Tupperware containers so that we could eat in the car going from one practice to another. The sports were always something I wanted to do. I wasn't going to just sit there and watch my brother do them!

"As it turned out I think ballet and gymnastics really helped my golf game. At the time it was just doing the things I wanted to do. I was in Olympic development gymnastics from 5:30 to 9:30 a minimum of 24 hours weekly. All that stuff also cut into my time as I got older and I picked golf. But I believe I am better for it."

"It really wasn't that crazy. We probably could have done a better job keeping the shrubs up but our house was really just a place to sleep. We didn't take family vacations. My children have never even been to Disney World. But the concept remained the same, we believed in exposing them to things.

"However we also explained to them if they were going to ask the family to spend money on what they wanted to do, they were going to have to do their best. It was their responsibility to do their stuff everyday as they grew into teenagers. She always seemed to really enjoy it."

"Have you practiced golf for 10,000 hours?"

"I am probably pretty close."

"If you believe in the idea of cross breeding sports she definitely has."

"Can you define your practice over the years? Tell us how you went about it?"

"Coming up, I spent much more time on the course. Then I went through a period where I spent a lot more time on the range. I think I got better for a while on the range working on mechanics but it got to a point of diminishing returns. In college, I should have spent more time on the golf course.

"It was really cut in two halves. Growing up, I spent more time playing. Then it became more practice. Now it is a balance of the two. I make sure there is a reason for what I do."

"Did you receive instruction growing up?"

"In golf, yes I did. My Dad exposed me to the game early. Dave Moskal, Robbi Richling, Rod Johnston, Steve Bryztwa, and Pam Stefanik all helped me. Mic Potter, my coach at Alabama, served two roles as instructor and coach. Outside of golf, I had a lot of good instructors though. Joanne Morscher and Dee Hillier were two of my biggest influences. My gymnastics instructors were my mental trainers now that I look back on it."

"Did you learn more than you were instructed?"

"Yes. Definitely. The first real instruction I got was from Rod Johnston."

"When did golf become instinct?"

"I would say my sophomore year in college. It surfaced here and there but I really didn't get the hang of it until I was in college."

"In the beginning, it was the sheer joy of doing what she wanted to be doing which was hitting a golf ball. It was because she was such a perfectionist that she became mechanical. Now, it is back to instinctive. I believe it was more immediate that golf was instinctive."

"When did you know what you wanted to be?"

"As long as I can remember I wanted to play golf. Why? I don't know. It just was…………"

Notable Achievements:
- **NCAA 1st Team All-American honorable mention**
- **SEC 1st Team honoree**
- **2 time champion on LPGA Futures Tour**
- **2012 LPGA Tour Rookie**
- **Futures Tour Player of The Year**

¿Hablas el idioma de los Campeones?

Introduction.

How should I speak to my children? Should I praise them for their accomplishments, or for their work ethic? Do I want my junior golfer to love learning or love winning? This chapter introduces some key terms: Fixed Mind-Set, Growth Mind-Set, and The Language of Champions. This chapter provides a new understanding of just how important Your words are to your junior golfer.

How many times have you heard this phrase: "It is not what you say, but how you say it." From helping people hour after hour, I know and understand things about the somewhat complicated game of golf. To succeed in helping people, I genuinely understand that it is not what I say, it is how I say it. One of the most difficult aspects of conveying a message is putting your message in the right terms for your intended audience. It takes time to learn this skill. As a parent, it is worth your time to hone this skill.

I have also been around people that are very good at this game and people that are very bad at this game. I have been around hard-headed people that were really good at golf. I have been around hard-headed people that were quite bad at golf. Trust me, you will also find open-minded people good at this game and closed-minded people good at this game. There is not a perfect brain among great players. Great players have many different personality characteristics. To communicate with great players, however, you do need to speak their language.

An Interpretation of Hogan's Quote.

So what is the language of champions? What is coming into their ears that makes them hear differently from the rest of the players? Why is it that some kids get extremely angry on the driving range and some do not? Why do some excel and some do not?

> **"My family wasn't rich, they were poor. I feel sorry for rich kids now, I really do. Because they are never going to have the opportunity I had. Because I knew tough things and I had a tough day all my life. And I can handle tough things, they can't. And every day that I progressed was a joy to me. And I recognized it every day."**
>
> **—Ben Hogan**

Mr. Hogan's point wasn't about being rich or poor. After all, at the time of this interview he was very wealthy himself. He had spent his adult life at the best golf clubs in the world. His friends were mostly prominent businessmen. Mr. Hogan also understood that money was vital to getting chances. Just look at any of the books about Mr. Hogan and you will see that a successful businessman named Marvin Leonard played a key role in his development. Mr. Hogan is not saying that kids from wealthy families cannot handle things like kids from a poor family. I am sure he had seen successful kids on both side of the fence. This is what I interpret Mr. Hogan saying:

"My family wasn't something special, we were just getting our feet under us. I feel sorry for kids that come from families that have already been really successful, I really do. Because they are never going to have the opportunity to learn the way I did. My family knew how tough things could be and nearly every day for my family was hard. I can handle tough days because I know I can learn from them. I don't have to live up to someone else's standard for me. Every day that I got to learn something was a joy to me. And I was thankful for being able to learn every day."

The further I travel down the road of being a golf instructor, the more I see one clear difference. **Children that enjoy learning do much better than children than enjoy being good at the game**. With an adolescent, you can sometimes see the boundaries go up around them. You can see they expect the good shots, are annoyed by average shots, and have difficulty receiving instruction. Many times, this same child was extremely hungry for knowledge only years before. What could have happened?

Of the 50 or so High School State Champions I have instructed, they are predominantly from middle class families. Does this mean that wealthy parents give their children everything while middle class families make their children work for it? My experience working with people from all socio-economic backgrounds does not point to this conclusion. In fact, viewed correctly, having monetary means only helps the child do more. But, there does seem to be a tipping point and I think Mr. Hogan knew it instinctively. I think nearly everyone understands it instinctively.

Do you want to be great? Do you really want to be great? How would it feel to be the very best golfer on the Earth? Remember, now that you are #1 there is nowhere to go except (you probably just said it) down. That is part of the intrigue with Tom Brady, Tiger Woods, Jack Nicklaus, or Michael Jordan just to name a few. They did not seem to be bothered (or scared) about being #1.

I recommend that you read some articles and books by Dr. Carol Dweck. She is a Stanford University psychologist that has researched many questions about a child's aptitude for learning. Essentially, she defines two types of people: Fixed-Minded and Growth-Minded. To me, her premise is simple: Fixed minded people will avoid being shown up by opportunities to learn; Growth minded people will steer INTO learning opportunities. This summary might be a gross over-simplification of her work, but I think it gets the point across. Of course, everyone exhibits instances of being Fixed-Minded and Growth-Minded.

My first recollection of being fixed minded was with my father and motorcycles. He loved them. A full day out riding motorcycles through trails just couldn't be topped for him. While a sense of adventure did appeal to me when I was young, I really did not truly enjoy riding motorcycles. But a boy will follow his father and I rode.

The message my father sent was very clear to me. "Honey," he said, talking to my mother, "VJ's got it. You should have seen how well he did. He handled that bike like a veteran today." I was probably 9 or 10 years old at the time and I completely understood the situation. My father had just said I was good at riding a bike. There were no major mechanical breakdowns and the ride went as good as it could go. I had accomplished my mission. My father was proud of me because I had proved I could cruise the trails. Mission accomplished.

I was now labeled as a veteran. I didn't want to prove my father wrong so I had nowhere to go but down. At first, I felt a bit nervous riding the bike after that. He probably noticed my reluctance and started handing out advice. The advice was given kindly at first. Then it became more dynamic in its presentation. Eventually, it ended up with him chasing me down the road with a stick shouting for me to shift out of 2nd gear. I literally had the "yips" when it came to riding motorcycles! All this transpired over about a six-month period. One day, it seemed that he gave up on me riding bikes. What a great day for me—I was absolutely thrilled!

Here is what happed. He praised me for my ability. I was convinced I was really good at riding a motorcycle. Then, I began to second-guess myself some because I didn't want to make an error that would prove him (or me) wrong. I made errors and then I got advice. But I didn't think I needed the advice because I was already full of ability. I thought I (the veteran) was letting us both down. The advice caused more second-guessing (outcome-oriented thinking) and his advice became more dynamic in its presentation. At this point, I had completely fallen from grace. I was no longer a veteran, I was a dip-s?$t that was making basic mistakes. I had lost it all. How was that possible? Now I just wanted out.

Was my dad wrong to say what he said to my mom? Come on, he was bragging on me! Am I a mental midget that can't learn? Come on, I accomplished many things after the motorcycle days. So what went wrong? Well that incident occurred because I was praised (and embodied that praise) for being "a veteran" when, in truth, I was really just a beginner. If I had heard my father say: "Your son really gave it a lot of effort today. He has a lot to learn, but I think he enjoys it," then I would have probably looked at motorcycling much different.

I have made the same mistakes as a father, too. On the 12th hole of our home course, on July 4th, 2009 my 7 year son made a hole-in-one from the women's tee. He took out his little blue driver, hopped on the tee, swung, and made it. It was unreal. People all around the club talked about it saying things like, "I didn't have my first one until I was 40!" or "I have never made on!" What did I say to my son? "You are different. You are going to make more hole-in-ones than them." Oops!

Dr. Carol Dweck: Praise Effort.

Dr. Carol Dweck has argued over and over again that praising our children for effort is better than praising them for an innate quality. When our children are praised for effort, they are in control. They can be resilient, have time to grow, learn, and understand. When we praise our children for being the best or for being winners, we are praising an outcome. Our children are not in control of outcomes. Their time for growth, learning, or understanding is diminished **because they must now win as they learn**.

You want to hear one of the greatest ways to mess up a fellow golfer? As they are looking over a putt, casually say: **"You haven't missed a putt that short in years."** This phrase resonates with the Fixed-Minded person that resides in us all. Suppose you are the one who hears this "encouragement" from one of your regular playing partners. What happens as soon as they say it? You immediately feel some emotion, or begin to hear some voices don't you? This saying sends the fixed-minded part of your brain a clear message: "You are a great putter. If you miss this one, well, your streak will be broken." What generally happens next?

While telling your children that they are the best might sound like a helpful way to grow their confidence, such words really work in the opposite way. Such high praise can set up a situation where your child will actually go out of their way to be the best. This means they can miss a critical step in the evolution of becoming great, which is getting beaten. It can lead to them being envious of other players' success. It can lead to a child that sees instruction as criticism. It can lead them to become defensive when the going gets tough. Eventually, it can lead to them giving up on the game.

So my question is: Why do parents tell their children they are special? Why do parents feel it to be necessary to tell their children that they are the best? Why do parents praise accomplishments? Of course, parents are generally quite proud of their children. The focus of your praise to your child, however, should be on learning, not on accomplishing.

While telling your children that you are proud of them for having the will to learn might not seem fruitful in the beginning, it could be the cornerstone to create confidence in your child. Praising your child's will to learn can set up situations where your child will actually seek to be tested. This search means that your child will learn that being beaten in a competition is a part of the learning process. This search also means that they will learn from the success of other players. This focus also can lead to a situation where a child that sees instruction as an opportunity to learn more. Finally, such a focus means your child will embrace being challenged when the going gets tough.

Young junior players with a fixed mind-set do not see effort as a desirable quality. They think: "Effort is for those that were not born great." I see this mind set quite often in our teaching center. These children believe they were born with an innate quality that places them above and beyond their competition. Effort, to them, is for other people. "He gets it really quick!" would be the parent's comment even before the child actually "gets it." You must understand that anyone that learns anything quickly understands the process of how to learn. A PGA Tour player might "learn" something quickly, but rarely, if ever, will a young junior golfer learn quickly when they are building motor skills.

Because the fixed mind-set junior player believes effort is for other players, they often fight taking control of the process. The word "process" implies effort, doesn't it? If there is no process, there is no plan. If there is no plan, then there is no deliberate effort. To me, the lack of a process is the most disabling aspect of the fixed mind in junior golf. If your junior golfer will not get involved in the process, they are asking to be devoured by the outcome.

In the end, the fixed mind-set junior player finds success with only winning or accomplishing external goals. Obviously, in golf this is a dead end street. Even the most elite golfers win only a small percentage of the time as they go from the different learning and competitive phases. An early start in golf can lead to multiple wins when everyone else is learning to play, but; as your young junior leaves their small pond they will find many other golfers who are equally skilled.

Young junior players with a growth mind-set see effort as a desirable quality. They see that pushing themselves daily changes the way they eventually putt or swing. They see the ball fly better or roll well as a by-product of their effort. I do my best to teach this mind set in my shop. Effort to them is what will create their success. The reason you don't see PGA Tour players standing on the range for five hours is because they are practicing by objectives, not time. Remind your growth mind-set juniors that your desire is that they practice with an objective. Set the objective in practice, accomplish it, and then go play.

Because the growth mind-set junior views effort as a desirable quality, they get involved in the process. The process in golf is mental, strategic, physical, technical, and nutritional. Often times, you will see some of the best juniors re-arranging their bags, cleaning their clubs, marking their ball a certain way, etc. It looks a bit "OCD" or at least "superstitious," but the reality is these activities are simply an offshoot of the process. At elite levels, the process means more than the win because the win is a by-product of the process.

In the end the growth mind-set junior finds success with objective effort and accomplishing internal goals. I whole-heartedly believe this is what Mr. Hogan is saying in his quote above. The process becomes the primary focus. The art of learning is self-taught via a process that makes growth the true goal.

So how do we all create a child with lofty goals, while living in a nurturing environment? Well, the first thing I always do is to listen. I listen to children. I listen to their body language, to their words, to their eyes, and to their actions. You should know that becoming a good listener takes many, many hours of (deliberate) practice. Begin by reminding your children that you are proud of their daily effort. Remind your children that you will let them go to tournaments or let them take lessons only if they put in the "behind the scenes" effort needed to work on their objectives. If I can get a child and parent to be accountable off the course to do their deliberate practice, we are on the right track.

The Golf Course.

Let's look at actually being on the golf course. Now, things get a little tricky. It is true that score is all that matters on the course. You simply must, however, instill the belief into your child that score is a by-product of a good process. On the course, make the routine the primary objective. Let them know that sometimes when they go play the conditions might be set against them. They might not shoot the lowest number of their life today but they will have the opportunity to practice their routines each time out. They will have the chance, hole after hole, to laugh at the emotions and go through their routines. They will have the chance to learn how a ball comes out of wet Bermuda grass. Every day on the course can either be a exhibition of emotional hijacking or an opportunity to place trust in their routine and the deliberate practice underlying the routine.

Basically, you should cultivate the notion that the golf course is also a **great place to learn about golf.** Avoid thinking that the golf course is only a place to score or win tournaments. Teach your children, through words and actions, the golf course is a place where they can experience the sport and learn many things needed to grow as a player. Stay away from the mindset that a course is only a place to judge their understanding of the sport. Tournaments are the judge of how well a golfer understands the game. My thinking is this: The golf course is a place for growth: mental, emotional, strategic, and mechanical.

As your child and you are building a growth mind-set, you must be aware of how to "layer the process." You layer the process with specific physical activities that enhances your child's golf swing and body. You layer the process with a more defined routine. You layer the process with deliberation in their practice. Just layer and layer, but do it while you are not judging their talent. Instead, judging, reward, and encourage their growth in the process. Applaud them for their daily practice. Applaud them for playing six holes running their routines. Applaud them for nearly any effort that has an objective.

I realize that you are most likely looking for a disciplined, but loving, environment for your child to learn about golf. This environment will not appear over night. Moreover, it will never appear if you place external achievements above internal growth. Keep it simple. Expect full participation, mentally and physically, in a developmentally appropriate process.

My father always goes back to my boxing days. Over the course of writing this book, we discussed many things. He says time and time again that when I was boxing was when I went from a mediocre soccer player to a "coach's 1st choice." He says it was when I went from an average tennis player to "a player with some aggression." He says it was when I went from a little guy swinging a club to "a club champion."

Whether the mental toughness of facing someone in the ring changed me or whether the stimulus of movement hit my growth velocity at the right time will be a debatable point between us for some time. To me, this is what really happened. VJ Trolio started believing that he could get better at something that he never thought he could even begin to tackle. I started noticing that the more I hit that bag, the easier it was for me to perform in the ring. I took control of a process for the first time and my life changed.

You must understand that it will be difficult to watch your children fail. I'm like you. It is not fun for me so see my children in tears. It is not easy for me to explain to my children they are not the best in the world. Not that these things occur daily, but we all face tough moments like these. There will be a constant tug at your chest (that is where emotion is felt) when you see your child fail. Parenting, like aging, is simply not for cowards. Be courageous and think differently. Be courageous by telling your children that their failing just means that their process needs to be tighten up a little bit. Be courageous and tell them they are expected to give full effort in the preparation for a tournament. Give them the courage to let the tournament decide the winner. If you are going to speak the language of champions, you must learn it. So go ahead, be courageous and LEARN!

In closing I want to address one more observation I have made over the years. "Well Johnny just likes team sports. He likes being a part of a team." Hogwash! Every child wants to be special, really special. They dream of it! Team sports, however, are a great place for a child with a fixed mind-set to hide. Just go ask coaches of team sports and they will tell you how difficult it is to keep the team competing as a unit. One of their biggest tasks is to keep the super-stars simply doing their own job on the field.

If a child is not using all their potential or is having a bad day, golf is the worst sport in the world to play. You, as parents, will probably hear some of this. Over the years, there will be times when football or softball will pop up for no apparent reason.   There is absolutely nothing wrong with team sports. After all, you and I are a part of a team every day at work aren't we? Just try to examine the situation and make certain that you child's mind-set is not driving the desire to play team sports. You must work to extinguish the fixed mind-set as soon as you distinguish the fixed mind-set in your child. You must be prepared to do so many, many times.

Chapter Lessons:

- Children that enjoy learning do much better in golf than children that enjoy winning.
- Think about what it is that draws your compliments toward your children.
- Be courageous: watch your children fail and teach them to focus on the process.
- Fixed mind-sets are created quickly. You must extinguish them as quickly as you distinguish them.

INSIGHTS

The insights of this young player will especially interest you. He is not only one of the best players I have ever instructed, but he is also one of the best people I have worked with in golf. Those who didn't understand just how good his process was were blown away when he reached the top of the collegiate rankings. For those of us that really knew him, his success was a by-product of a process that was planned many years ago. *His father's words are in italicized text.*

"How many sports did you play?"

"I played basketball, soccer, and baseball. Football, I played for one year. Soccer camps in the summer, but I was best at baseball. I was a really good position player, playing all star and travel ball. When I was really little, I did gymnastics for three or four years and even a little piano. I hated reading music, so piano didn't last very long."

"He started into the big three (baseball, basketball, and football) as well as soccer, beginning with T-ball and city league soccer at age five or so. I think he preferred baseball and soccer from the others. Golf started at age four, when he rode in a cart with me and dropped a ball near mine on the course. He thought heaven had come to earth when, as a six year old, he completed his first nine hole round."

"When did you start playing golf?"

"I started playing golf at age four. Dad sawed down a Ben Hogan eight iron and a little putter. He would take me to the course and I would hit it and run down the fairways and pick up my ball. We would ride to his next shot, and I would do it again. Anything with a ball was my thing."

"At what age did you begin to specialize in golf?"

"My first tournament was in 1991 when I was ten. It was June 6th 1991, but I didn't really start specializing until I was twelve. Every other sport was done by age twelve. It happened all in a week really. One weekend I was playing in the state junior hitting snap hooks and the next weekend I was at a baseball tournament and couldn't hit a pitch because I was swinging up on it! That was enough for me. I was like 'forget this'."

"By the time he was nine, he was gravitating toward golf. By age twelve, he finally chose golf as his sole sport, having noticed his baseball swing was interfering with his ball striking."

"Was there a moment you said to yourself, 'Hey this is something I can do?"

"I knew Jake Lambert was good on a national stage. I knew I could get good. When I started playing a local city junior golf league, I couldn't sleep at night. That had never happened with another sport. My first tournament in this local city league, I shot 43 and won. That feeling made it "the game" above other sports.

At the same time, I began volunteering at our state's local PGA Tour event as a sign boy. I wanted to be one of those guys, so I figured I would do it. I didn't win any tournaments until I was twelve, and I think it might have had something to do with not being great at first. I was pretty good at everything else but golf was tough. I gravitated toward golf I think because there was so much more to the game than other games. As a child I was a Lego fanatic so putting a golf game together was, to me, exactly the same [as putting together a Lego figure]."

"Did you play or practice more as a youngster?"

"When I got to where I could hit it more than 100 yards, I played in a bunch of scrambles with my Dad. Pharmaceutical companies put on a lot of tournaments at different places back then and I got to play a ton because my Dad was invited to them. I was home schooled during the 3rd grade, so I had the afternoons clear to play golf. I just played and played.

"When I got to about age twelve, I started getting lessons and started practicing for the first time, really. Especially wedge practice. My early instructors were huge on the short game. So the time I did spend practicing was on the short game. I went from an absolutely middle of the road junior golfer to a pretty good one."

"Early on definitely more play than practice, although he had a real affinity for both. Practice became more deliberate at the encouragement of his first instructor at age ten."

"Overall, have you played more or practiced more?"

"Overall, I have done more practice probably than playing. In college, I would practice from 1pm till 5pm nearly every day. I would say that the emphasis is more heavy on practice these days. When I started getting serious about golf, my fundamentals were a little behind. So I had to do a lot of stuff my competition didn't have to do."

"The pendulum has swung steadily toward more practice, and it probably passed the midway point somewhere around the age of twelve. Now, he certainly practices more than he plays, probably a 3 to 1 ratio. One thing you should understand, it really wasn't about the score or about the minutia of mechanics at first. The golf course attracted him like a fish to water. The sights the sounds, the smells, the people, shoes, gloves, clubs and ball itself had a hold on him. He found his home and never left. For him the saying is really true, "Golf is Life – And The Rest Are Minor Distractions."

"Can you define your practice for us? Mirrors, drills, driving ranges, etc.?"

"Early on, up until I was 15, all I worried about was ball beating and ball flight. Dad would video me so I was accustomed to seeing myself on video. I have always been a pretty visual learner about my swing but I really had a skewed perception of it because I was hitting balls and trying to feel it.

"I gradually got more and more deliberate in my practice. I grew up on "the wee links" so my short game stuff was second hand by age 15 or 16. So, I started getting the right feedback from mirrors, or having something under my arm, or looking at a shadow. I started using more drills to be precise in the way I was doing stuff.

"More and more my practice got away from ball flight and more into what "I" was doing. Before I was trying to get in a "now" position. Now I practice with intent and purpose."

"He will reluctantly do what is asked of him that requires him to be away from the course (and then only until he conveniently forgets). He spends the bulk of his practice time on those drills that he can do on the range or chipping green or putting green. When time is tight, or the weather is unfavorable, he may not get on the course at all for several consecutive days.

"Practice includes a variety of drills which are geared toward sharpening the good or getting rid of the bad. In the past few years, he has been more

disciplined with process training and working on the correcting things, giving little regard for the outcomes. This change in focus was a really big hurdle for him as has always wanted the ball in the hole or the ball to fly correctly no matter what.

"As he nears time to compete, he gets away from concerns about mechanics and focuses more on scoring with the game he's got at the time. Importantly, he has learned that for every day he doesn't strike a ball, he will need a day to work to get back to where he was with his game. Needless to say, he rarely misses a day at the course."

"Do you think you have logged 10,000 hours of practice?"

"Yes, probably. Since 7th grade I have been at the golf course nearly every day from 3:00 till dark on the weekdays and nearly all day on Saturdays. In college it was even more. So yes, I have probably put in 10,000 hours. It has never been a burden though. "

"Come on, it has never been a burden?"

"Well at times—but, I would mix it up. In college, I would study at the golf house and do some drills, study, do some drills, study, etc. I always broke it up even at the range.

"How much instruction have you had over the years?"

"First lessons were at age ten. I had another instructor at age twelve and a third at age 15."

"His first lesson was at age ten. His coached just poured gas on the fire that was already in his heart, and he was overrun with excitement and anticipation. He has consistently taken lessons about every three to six weeks, twelve months a year since then."

"When did golf become 'instinctive' for you?"

"I think I have always had an instinct that I felt 'at home' on the course. It really became instinctive right before I won `The Bubba,' just before my junior year of high school. It has really been instinctive ever since then."

"I really think he was born with the instinct. At least you could say he was born with the predispositions and affinities that have resulted in golf fitting him like a glove; all the way from the intrigue of the impact of a particular milled pattern on his putter face to the energy acquired from 100 spectators watching around the 18th green. To some degree, you could say that parenting is about helping your child find his place in the world. I introduced him to a lot of places, but this one he embraced and hasn't let go."

"If you had to give advice to an aspiring junior golfer, what would it be?"

"Learn fundamentals and practice your short game. Play a bunch and have fun with it."

Notable Achievements:
- **State Amateur Champion**
- **State Junior Champion**
- **High School State Champion**
- **Semi-Finalist USGA Public Links**
- **1st Team All-American**
- **1st Team All-SEC**
- **Participant In 4 USGA Events**

Huh?

Some stories are worth telling. In a small southern town, there were two players, a U.S. KIDS World Champion and a USGA Championship Semi-Finalist. Such honors seem unlikely at first glance. According to a recent census, the population of the town is 4,032—1,835 females and 2,197 males. The estimated medium household income is $25,294. There is one golf course—with only nine holes.

The story begins with the birth of the only son of the golf course manager and his wife. The home they live in was nearly on the golf course itself—just like the homes of many club professionals in the rural south. At the age of three, the young boy began swinging a golf club. Whether it was from his close proximity to the course or his awareness of people swinging clubs all around him, his father thought the son "looked like a player when he started swinging." The young man's contact was good at age three. By the age of seven, he started getting serious about golf. In his first tournament, a recognized regional event, he finished 5th with only five clubs in the bag. He won his second tournament: The Pepsi Little People's, played in Illinois.

Close by, another father was charged with entertaining his three year old daughter most afternoons. This situation occurred because his wife was working an odd shift at the company. Because he was a golfer, this father decided that he would cut down a club (it was either a 3- or 7-iron) as a play toy for her. She immensely enjoyed hitting the little plastic balls in the backyard. She had so much fun that her father began to take her to the golf course with him when she was five year old.

The father of the young girl reported, "After seeing her for a while at the course, the golf course manager told me she had some talent." The seemingly "talented" little girl had honed her skills with the plastic balls in the backyard using her father's cut-down iron.

By age nine, the son of the golf course manager had accomplished an extraordinary feat. He won the U.S. KIDS World Championship. The tournament is likely the largest junior golf tournament in the world, hosting a field of over 1,200 players from 30 countries.

Both children grew up playing multiple sports. The young man played t-ball, baseball, golf, and a little junior high football. The young lady grew up with softball, basketball, and golf. She would get home from a weekend of softball tournaments and play in a golf tournament the next day. "I hate softball," her father remembers her saying.

The young man, on the other hand, decided reasonably early that golf was a better sport for him. "He told me at about seven years old that if I would take him to golf tournaments, he would back away from baseball," his father recalls. While the young lady continued to play basketball competitively throughout high school, the young man chose golf as his only competitive outlet. The young man played other sports, but more for fun than competitively. With the golf course in the backyard, the young man felt that golf was really just a way of life.

After three years of competition the young man had racked up 31 wins in tournament play. The start for the young girl wasn't quite as glorious. As her father recalls, "At about age twelve, she played in The Pepsi Little People's—her first national event. She was disqualified for a rules violation. It wasn't anything intentional; it involved a breach of the rules with a lost ball. Our whole family was there, ever her grandparents. We were all disappointed, but it was what it was."

One of the advantages she had, however, was the chance to follow the path of the slightly older young man. Her father recounts, "We went from playing the course, to playing a local tour, to playing the state's junior circuit. Being the only girl around in her age group was also an advantage. Nearly each time out, all the other competitors were boys. Also, the more she played in tournaments, the more she liked it."

My questions, of course, were "What lay behind the scenes?" How much did they practice and play?" The golf course manager replied, "We would do something five or six days a week. It might not be much, but it would be something." "Gradually, using their attention span as a guide, we would practice more. In his younger years, it was just the two of us. The young lady had not joined us. When he was young, we might just play four holes. Later on, if he could keep his attention, we might play be nine holes. We did a lot of drills in the house, too. I would say maybe 15 or 20 minutes worth three or four days a week."

"For her," recalls the young girl's father, "there was always a good bit of practice. Early on it was just fun. As she got older, she might spend about two hours a week working on her mechanics. Early on of course, there was some ball pounding on the range. But, as she got older, she became more deliberate about her practice. When her coach began to change her swing, there was a lot of mirror practice at home. To tell the truth, doing the drills was like pulling teeth. She hated having her score suffer on the golf course—so that helped her embrace the drills."

Looking back, the players recall it a bit differently. "I never really beat balls five or six hours a day," the now grown young man says confidently. "I guess it has always been more quality than quantity. My dad helped me practice correctly. Sometimes I have to think of things differently and he would always be out there helping me out."

"I did most of my drills at home and then I would go to the golf course," admits the now grown up young lady. "One year I had a bunch of drills marked down for the things I needed to do with my swing."

So how would two kids, one that had to be coached via his attention span and another that "doing drills was like pulling teeth," grow into two young adults that talk about quality versus quantity and embrace the idea of drills? The golf course manager held the secret.

"They were both so different," says the golf course manager. "She could stay out there all day long, but he could not. Practice for both of them was always as intentional and deliberate as I could make it. We didn't do anything with practicing ball flight. They were always working on their swings, not the ball flight. For them the ball flight or the score was not the instructor. I would sit back and watch them and I knew what they needed to do with their swings. Both of them received instruction and feedback on what they needed or on what they were doing. They bought into the process of building good motion. They trusted what their swing instructor and I were saying and learned not to take short cuts."

"In the past four years," recalls the father of the now grown up young lady, "she has become more and more deliberate in her practice. She played so many rounds and nearly all of them had a purpose. Her goal was pretty clear by age twelve: Play college golf and play on the LPGA Tour after that. We reminded her that reaching these goals meant that she would miss out on some things other children would be doing."

Carefully read and understand what the golf course manager said above: "They bought into the process of building good motion." The process of standing in front of the mirror and working on their motions were something they could control. Standing on the range and making good swings was something they could control. The golf course manager understood the process. "We always tried to use drills. As we progressed, eventually we would look at ball flight," recalls the young man. "I never really worried about ball flight until I got close to a tournament." The young girl says it like this, "Get your feel from drills. It is very important to know how the correct motion should feel before hitting a golf ball."

Both sets of parents created the template for success. They graded their children by how well they worked and how much they worked. The golf course manager tried to teach both children only when they were capable of listening. Recall that he used their attention spans as a guideline.

For parents who are constantly grading their children by their golf scores and ball flight, listen to the answers to the following question: "If you wanted to make a really bad junior golfer, what would you tell them?"

The young man's answer was: "I would tell them to worry about ball flight. The thing my Dad and I have always said is that we get our feel from mechanics instead of ball flight. I would also tell them to play all the time while worrying about the ball flight and trying to hit it correctly."

The young lady's answer to the same question was: "I would say practice all the time worrying about ball flight. The junior player will get tired by practicing all-day and they will get frustrated from the ball flight not being correct. I would also tell them to get the feel of their swing from ball flight."

My next question was: "If you wanted to make a great junior golfer what would you tell them?" The young man's answer was: "I would tell them to go out and play. Learn to get the ball around the course—no matter how good or bad. Then, I would tell them to get their feels from drills. Go in a progression with the swing." The young lady answered" "I would say play golf, but still do drills. Play, practice, and do drills in equal amounts. Practice, for me, is when I hit a golf ball. Drills are when there is no ball and I am concentrating on how I am moving. The drills make the practice and the practice makes the playing."

As you can imagine, knowing what to do but not doing it enough is really useless. My next question to them both was a simple one: "Have you (they) practiced 10,000 hours?" The golf course manager answered: "Yes. Easily. He has always been out there." The father of the young lady said, "Maybe not yet. It would be close to that adding in playing time, though." The young man replied: "Yes. I would say so. I miss a few days but I try not to. I try to do something every day. I haven't missed too many days." The young lady added: "I would probably be pretty close. It may not be over 10,000 hours. I never have thought that I had been out there that much. But when you throw the numbers at me I guess I have."

These two children grew up listening to a golf course manager that preached effort and doing your best. They were taught to practice and work on the things that they could control instead of on things that they could not control.

Both sets of parents created a culture of hard, steady work. Both children devoted countless hours working on the craft of perfecting the process of learning.

Their combined results:

- **4 individual State High School Championships (one of them accomplished by her playing against the boys)**
- **3 High School State Team Championships**
- **5 State Junior Championships**
- **1 US Kids World Championship**
- **8 Exxon/BFI Championships**
- **2 Pepsi Little People's Championships**
- **1 Women's State Amateur Championship**
- **1 Trusted Choice Big "I" National Championship**
- **1 USGA Semi-finalist**

But the question still lingers in this story, "Why?" Why did this all happen in such a short span and in such a small town?

"It was the golf course manager," says the young lady's father. "He saw something in my daughter and said so repeatedly. He convinced us to have her start playing in competition. He would always be saying something about how good she could be." The golf course manager remarked, "I had confidence in the kids, in the swing instructor, and I enjoyed watching them get better and I knew they could get even better! I always believed that if you work hard at whatever it is you are doing, you can get really good at it. They outworked 90% of the others, but worked with intent. To me, it was just being honest with the kids. A lot of it is being truthful—good or bad. Once they realize you are just being honest with them it gets easier. A lot of the parents were really result oriented. I don't know if parents are lying to their children or just don't know the truth."

When the players were asked why they chose golf, the young man said, "I love it. Secondly, it is my lifestyle. I like going to different places and competing with everyone." The young lady answered, "I have had a goal for years. I know the highest-level players work hard. I might not be the most talented, but I know if I work hard I can get there. There have been some sacrifices, but I am willing to do that. It helped to have people around me that encouraged me. The golf course manager, my swing instructor, and the people around me were all telling me that I could be great. It helps to know that people see your potential."

In this story, it is easy to see how the hard work came together. As children matured, their attention spans governed the teaching time. As they learned, the emphasis was put on them, not the ball flight or score. Both kids commented on how their parents have never gotten on to them for a physical error on the course. Only mental errors were pointed out—because the players had control over their decisions. Both of the kids commented they were not worried about ball flight during practice sessions. They were worried about moving correctly. Both players were raised in a culture that praised effort and approaching the game correctly—results were simply results. Both of them put in thousands of hours of intentional practice. When asked what they were thinking about when they played, both of them said, "Our routines, mostly. We always use playing to work on our routines."

But something else also happened. The golf club got involved. The older men at the club followed the kids' exploits in golf. Pictures of the kids adorned the walls of the pro shop. The golf club began to take pride in how well the children were doing. Kids from neighboring towns began to win big events around the state. It seems that not only did the children learn a great process, but they also gave other kids the belief they could do it too.

In closing I asked them all, "Do you think what was accomplished by these two players will ever happen again?" All four respondents began the answer with deep sighs. It was really quite humorous to hear! One commented "Whooooo! I don't think so, not in the near future." Another said, "I hope so, but it will be hard." Still another said, "No. I really don't see anybody at our age doing what we did."

But I think the young lady summed it up the best. "I want to say there is a possibility, but I don't know. With the people I see around, golf is not really a sport anyone is interested in. There are kids that come out, but they are not really serious. I don't really know why we pursued golf the way we did. I guess just because.....I don't really know why it happened. I guess you could say God put us here and that was it."

The name of this chapter, "HUH…" comes from what most people say when they learn the identity of the town where these two are from. "Huh? Where now?" would be the common question back. The moral of this story is simple. Facilities and equipment do not build champions. People build champions.

Even though the moral of the story generally is the last part of a story, I want to add some additional quotes from the interviews as an epilogue. I hope you enjoy them as much as I did.

What are the biggest stumbling blocks for parents?

"There is a line. You can't be too nice, but you can't stay constantly pissed at them either. The worst I have seen is on the course when the parents get mad at their children."

"I know they want their kids to do really well, but they push them too hard in performance. My dad pushed me to practice, not really to perform. With playing, he never got on to me for what I physically did wrong. He always reflected on what I was thinking about when I hit the shot. When I would get lazy, he would remind me to do my drills. It was never really the performance side."

When did golf become instinctive?

"Wow. I really don't know. She really loved golf from the beginning. Really, she was gifted early to a point where she would relax and play. At about age 14, she thought she was supposed to win. I would say that little girl in the back yard hitting balls was doing it instinctively. How do you explain that? My explanation is that it is God given."

"I don't know if it is completely instinctive now. They are still learning. They had a little bit of golfing talent but they worked so hard. When we go back and look at their swings of age eight or ten compared to the swings now, it isn't even close. When they were growing up, people would say to me, 'Why do you want to take him to a golf guru and screw up their swing.' They just didn't understand."

What do you think the single biggest factor in creating these two golfers?

"I think so much of it was him having played in the junior events really young and having success. He had won the US Kids by age 10 or so. When she started, she had mentors to keep something ahead of her. As an 8th grader, she and the other girls on the high school team won their first time out. He had things going for him early that made him believe he could really play with anybody. I don't think she really knew how good she was until she made it to the US Junior Semi's."

"Fundamentals. The fundamentals of playing, of their mechanics, and of their minds grew together. It wasn't ball flight or scores. It was more the process of integrating fundamentals. I say process, process, and process all the

time to them. In 2007, they won their first state championship. A guy was there giving a book away. We used a lot of stuff from the book, **_7 Days At The Links of Utopia._** *Focus on the present. All we can control is what we are doing right now. Don't get ahead of yourself, and don't look back. They do a wonderful job of staying in the present—staying in the present begins with practice."*

What would be your normal day in the summer time?

"Get up at 7:30 or 8:00. Go out and hit balls for an hour. Go putt and chip. Take a break. Then I would go play nine holes. Take a break. Work around the greens some more. I will be at the course all day but it is not practice, practice, all day. Mentally, I can't go full bore from sunrise to sunset. I know what I am going to work on every day before I go out. For a while it was my hips, and when I am on the golf course, I always go through my routine. No matter what is happening on the course, I am repeatedly going through my routine on the course."

"Get up around 8:30. I would be at the course by 10:00. I would drill and practice for a couple of hours. Then lunch. Get loose and then go play 9 or 18 holes. Normally after I play I focus on what I didn't do well and I would go work on it for 1 hour or so. A day would last from 10:00 till 6:00 or so."

"I Am Going to Disney World"

Introduction.

Golf lessons and diets don't work for the same reason. It is easy for a child to feel entitled, as we all know. However, sometimes we need to look around at what we are providing. Are we feeding entitlement or making our children earn experiences? This chapter introduces you to a key concept: The Habit Calendar. This chapter will completely explain the process of using a habit calendar and some drills that have built a really great base for junior golfers. It will open your eyes to a different "way" of practice with a method that has been proven effective time and time again.

Most everyone can remember the answer to Walt Disney World's famous TV commercial at the end of the Super Bowl. If you do not remember, the commercial was simple. The football player was asked: "You just won the Super Bowl! What's next?" The player would joyously shout to the camera, "I am going to Disney World!"

Disney World is really appealing to children. Rewards come easy at Disney World. Kids can eat cookies at 10:00 am and probably get away with it. Kids can devour ice cream for lunch and parents will allow it. There is visual stimulus everywhere, and adventure around every corner. Everyone is welcome to be a part of something special.

In sports, however, not everyone is welcome to be a part of something special. Sure, you can be a fan of a great organization but that will not make you a player. Sure, you can get lessons from the best instructor but that will not guarantee anything but the best information. Being a part of something great requires disciplined, sustained, and correct work. It is really that simple.

Let's survey our children's lives for a second. Mine each have an iPod Touch, loaded with Apps and games. The iPad Santa brought was supposed to be for "educational" Apps only, but now college football games rule. When they start a fire, they do it with a starter log. They have a 35-inch television, teddy bears, a Play-Station, dozens of footballs, swords, a tight rope in the back yard, bikes, trikes, skateboards. We scrimped and saved to buy a house in a neighborhood that is safe for our children.

How about the experiences we provide for our children? Our family does not go to many places (maybe the beach once or twice each year). Often times, my wife and I feel like we, as parents, should do more for our children. Sure, we have been "out West" and, of course, to Disney World, but we feel compelled to take our children to other places for "the experience." In fact, as I look around at our children's lives, I see more items they don't use than ones they do use. Is this normal? Or am I creating a Disney World on a middle class budget?

The harsh reality is that if we keep this pace up, our children might not have time to become great at anything. They will be too busy "experiencing" things to settle in and begin the slow steady art of becoming great at something. Moreover, when we want our children to "go to karate" they, of course, don't like it. When we demand that they go to their rooms and "study," they put up a fight. Of course, if my wife forbids me to eat ice cream while at Disney World, I would get upset pretty quickly. Wouldn't you?

Disney World is a wonderful place, but its experience should not be lived everyday by children that want to be great at a specific sport. Giving you 13 year old a speech on discipline while you play video games with him or her probably will not result in increased discipline. Sending them to their room to work on their putting strokes with a television sitting on the chest of drawers will probably lead to a lack of deliberate practice. Texting constantly on the golf course and then expecting your child to focus on their routines will probably lead to problems down the road.

At the same time, taking out the gas stove and installing a wood burning one probably isn't the greatest idea either. Throwing the video games in the garbage and handing your nine-year old son a wood splitter will probably cause some problems. Taking your daughter's high heels from her closet and replacing them with golf shoes will, no doubt, throw some gasoline on a fire with the ladies in the house.

Diets don't work for a reason. People eat out of convenience and they get fat. At some point, they get so fat they must lose weight. A big problem, however, with squeezing in the workout and changing the diet is that these activities are so far from the normal routine that the individual cannot sustain these activities. So, the diet falls by the way side and the person goes back to eating the way they did in their normal routine.

Golf lessons don't work for a reason. People practice out of convenience and they don't shoot the scores they wish. A big problem, however, with squeezing the extra practice time and changing the swing is so far from the normal routine that the individual cannot sustain these activities. So, the lesson falls by the way side and the person goes back to playing and practicing as they had before the lessons.

Responsibility and relevance work hand in hand. When a child grows up in "Disney World" is suddenly asked to give me 1,000 reps of a certain drill and play 45 holes weekly before their next lesson, they look at me with a confused expression.

Note that I am not passing judgment on what happens in your home in any way. Instead, I want to lay out a plan that you can implement that will take your child from "Disney World" to the "Battlefield" in stages that can be accomplished. So, no worries, you can keep the air-conditioning and TVs plugged in (for now).

Years ago I was on a research mission. I wanted to know everything there was to know about impacting a golf ball and thinking one's way around a golf course. **The focus of my research now is on what will lead to the biggest gains in performance.** What I have also learned is those who are the best at this game are interested in ways to improve performance. They aren't interested in being a lab rat. They want to play better golf.

One evening I was sitting in a hotel with a player and we were talking golf. "Why do you teach?" he asked. I replied, "Because this game really makes me angry. People think I love golf, but I don't. I want to beat the game." Laughing, he replied, "VJ, you can't beat this game. You can only steal moments from it, and hope you are putting for a million dollars when you do." Maybe he is right. Maybe the game cannot be beaten, but there are some ways that are better than others when it comes to stealing moments from this game.

Over the years, there are definitely ways that lead to bigger gains with developing golfers. The former chapters were laid out for that reason. If you will stick to them you will see some huge gains in your children's golf games and possibly yours. This chapter contains some physical and mental drills that have worked beautifully for many different players. We are going to lay out the path to ease out of "Disney World" and onto the "Battlefield!"

The Habit Calendar

December 2011						
Sunday	Monday	Tuesday	Wednesday	Thursday	Friday	Saturday
				1	2	3
4	5	6	7 Pearl Harbor Remembrance Day	8	9	10
11	12	13	14	15	16	17
18	19	20	21 Winter Begins	22	23	24
25 Christmas	26	27	28	29	30	31 New Year's Eve

    A centerpiece of instruction for juniors is the habit calendar. It is where the children earn instruction. It is where they earn new equipment. It is where they earn golf balls. The habit calendar should be put in a centralized area of the home, a place where everyone can see it. The "team" (parents and the child) determines an amount of time or a number of reps that should be done daily. The child performs the reps daily and puts an "X" (or whatever they wish) to show the task has been completed.

    Pictured above is an example of a child's habit calendar. For a child to create good fundamentals in their golf swing, they must move. Remember, swing changes happen at a cellular level, not a cognitive level. Therefore, it is imperative they not only work on their swing, but they do it often. Furthermore, the skill of becoming responsible for preparing for an event is a learned behavior just like hitting a chip shot is a learned behavior. The habit calendar is the beginning of this **Process**.

    The habit calendar above is from a seven year old. He practices a particular element of his swing three minutes each day. At the end of 60 days, he has earned another lesson or golf balls or some type of reward. I often use the habit calendar as a calculator too. This seven year old worked on "shortening his swing" for 60 days—and he even did so on Christmas day! The total time devoted was 180 minutes. You can use the calendar to show your child that doing a little bit every day really adds up.

The habit calendar can eventually go away. Sooner than later, you will see a child that feels compelled to work on their swings, or their putting, or their chipping each day. By holding them accountable in the beginning, you are teaching them to hold themselves accountable in the end. This accountability puts a premium on preparation. Before the habit calendar goes away (more than likely it will be around for a number of years), it will be adjusted to work on all elements of the game. At some point, a very mature point, time will no longer matter. Instead the player will practice with intentions that probably cannot be measured with time alone. I should confess, however, that to this day, I personally practice using a habit calendar.

Fundamental Drills.

BALL POSITION

Ball Position is a fundamental element to the golf swing. I often remark that ball position can be either a tempter or a teacher. For a young player, ball position is an important fundamental to create a nice weight shift from one leg to the other in a consistent sequence. As golfers improve, ball position hugely affects the path of the club and the curve of the ball. Eventually, a laundry list of swing "complications" can be traced back to the fundamental element of ball position.

For youngsters, my preference is definitely a forward ball position. Two golf balls inside the left heel is acceptable for the beginner, and ball position will become more and more important as they continue in the game. The reason is simple. If the ball position is constant, the weight shift can be consistent. The exercise is simple. Address the ball over and over (for a pre-determined amount of time/reps each day) making certain the ball is positioned two golf balls inside the left foot.

BALL POSITION + BODY POSITION

A bit more advanced way of learning ball position can be done using a mirror. Here the junior sets up to a ball that is played two inches inside the left heel (the center of the ball) and they also get their body in a neutral position. A neutral position means that their shoulders, hips, knees, and ankles are stacked on top of one another. As a result of this neutral position, the ankles bear the weight of the knees, the knees bear the weight of the hips, and the hips bear the weight of the shoulders. This neutral position will place the neck between the feet.

Again, this drill is simple. Walk into your stance looking at the ball—just as you would when you are addressing the ball on the range. Once set, look into the mirror. Check ball position, neck position, and joints. Repeat. It only takes a glance to see whether your child is not in a neutral position. Then, of course, you can them see the compensation and make an adjustment. Repeat for the desired amount of time or reps.

GRIP

     A junior golfer's grip will change and change and change! I have found really no rhyme or reason for it. Generally, the trail hand will get a little under the shaft or the lead hand will get a little too far on top of the shaft. Whatever the case, too strong of a lead hand will inevitably cause a shut face and a digging tendency around the greens. A trail hand too far under the shaft will generally cause a less than desirable wrist release pattern, especially around the greens. Keeping the grip as neutral as possible and as consistent as possible will be a time saver later on in their golfing careers.

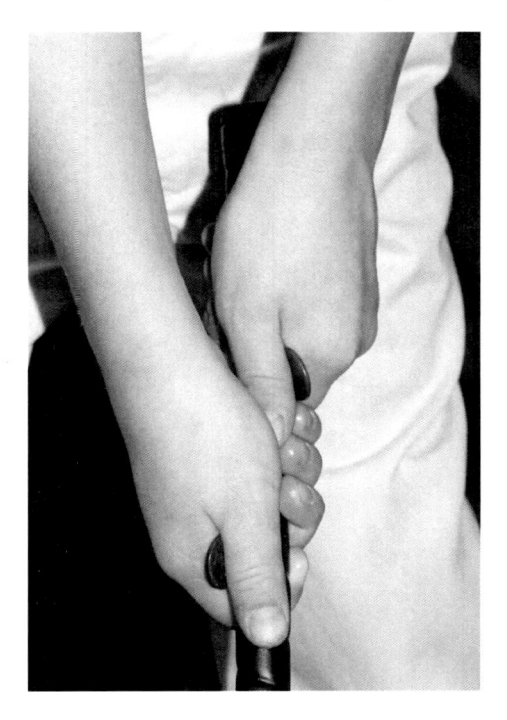

     This drill, or exercise, is generally done sitting on the couch. Again, it is very simple. The goal is to have the "v" formed between the thumb and index finger point (essentially) to the rear shoulder. My preference is for the children to hold a coin between the thumb and index finger because it serves multiple purposes later on. With that said, they simply put their hands on the club, note that they are properly placed, and waggle the club a bit. Take the hands completely off the club, and repeat the same task for the desired amount of time or reps.

WEIGHT SHIFT

Much of my personal research on the golf swing revolves around two aspects of the golf swing: Ball position and weight shift. Ball position and weight shift are strongly related. They might even be thought of as inseparable. Every ball position requires a corresponding weight shift to send a ball flying to the target. To ensure, or at least promote, a "healthy" weight shift, ball position is critical. Often times, it is important to come in behind ball position and work specifically on weight shift.

Using a standard mirror and electrical tape create a vertical line down the mirror. Have your child address an imaginary ball with the vertical line cutting the body in half from the perspective of a sagittal plane. Starting with the head on the line, go to the top of the swing. Nothing should have moved too far from the line. Next go to the finish. Here your child should have their rear ends in front of the line and the head/neck should still be "essentially" in the same place. Repeat for the prescribed amount of reps or time.

In my world, primary and secondary tilts of the spine are very important. For consistent ball striking, a youngster must learn how to shift their lower body through the ball without having any jerky motion with their upper torso. I can't tell you the number of young golfers that must learn to work on stabilizing the body through the strike of the ball!

PITCHING/CHIPPING ON ONE LEG

Accurate pitching and chipping requires stabilization. In other words, junior golfers need to learn the minimum movement necessary to get the job done. This drill is really important for junior golfers because, at the junior golf level, getting the ball up and down is an enormously important aspect of scoring.

Setting up this drill is simple. The youngster will be using a chipping or pitching motion while on one leg. The lead leg will be the one they pivot around by simply picking of the trail leg and bending (at the knee) it behind them. Now they will go back and through, back and through with decent mechanics (no "wristy" throwing motions of the shaft through the hitting are) as they keep their balance.

Obviously, the shoulders will rotate a bit, and so will their hips. The lead knee and ankle will also swivel some. Any tilting back or lack of rotation will clean itself up. Performing this drill in front of a mirror is also helpful. Perform this drill the prescribed amount of reps or for the agreed upon time.

THE PUTTING STROKE

Two facets of the putting stroke are extremely important for making putts. The first one is to have some type of stroke where the club face and the swing path match. All too often in junior golf, we see considerable face rotation through the impact area. The results of this rotation can get deadly on those four footers! To help junior golfers build a motion, buy THE PUTTING ARC and set one up. The instructions are essentially fool proof and no ball is needed.

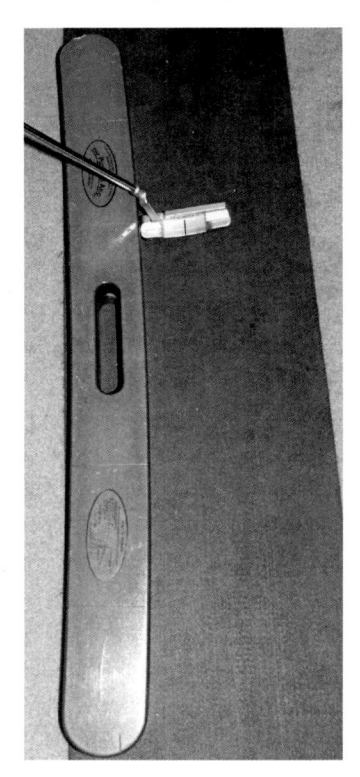

Have your child (and you too) address the arc and move the putter back and through while keeping the face parallel to the upper line and the heel of the putter while moving gently along the arc. Perform for the desired amount of reps or time period.

Secondly, kids will move their heads all over the place when they putt. To help them build a solid fundamental simply get an old CD out and toss it on the floor. Now have the child address an imaginary ball and position their heads so they can see their eyes reflecting back to them. Simply move the putter back and through the desired amount of reps or time period while maintaining the eye reflection.

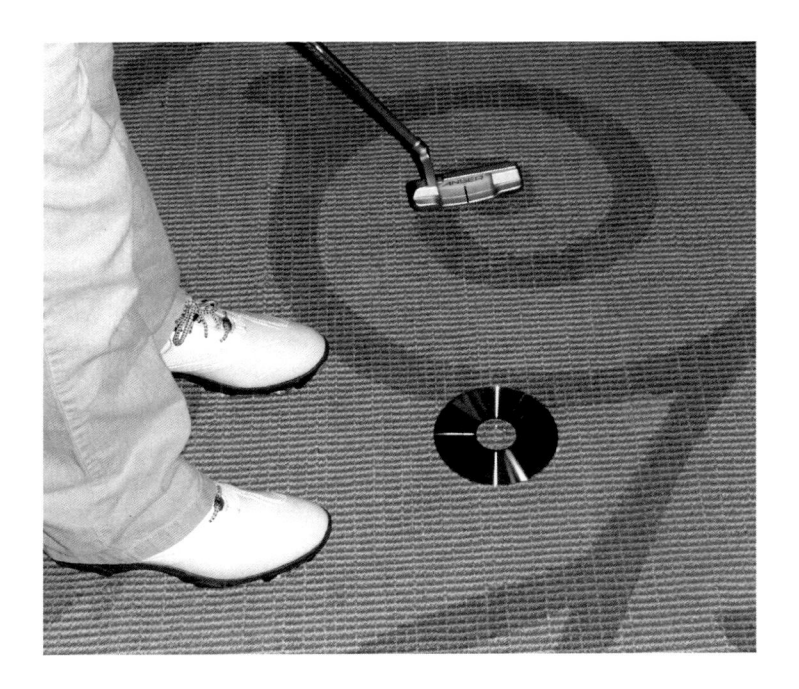

PLAY

    Forget the custom of playing nine or 18 holes of golf. Encourage them, bribe them, do whatever it takes to get them to the golf course and play a few holes—even in the worst weather. Whether it is three holes with a buddy or 18 holes with the club champion, playing golf regularly will lead to huge gains. Keep them on the course regularly and, more importantly, let them have fun playing golf.

    The pictures in this chapter were taken in our home for a reason. You don't need a fancy Teaching Center! You don't need a "golf room" dedicated to the sole purpose of improving the golf swing. All you need is some knowledge, motion, and intent. Utilizing these physical drills and the mental drills of proper practice is a big part of the foundation. **Trophies may be handed over at beautiful places but they are not earned there.**

    A very, very good foundation for a junior golfer to build upon is:

- A neutral ball position
- A weight shift that accommodates the ball position
- A steady head and a decent putting stroke
- A stable body when hitting chip shots

Even more important is for parents to cultivate a deeply held belief that motion is necessary for junior golfers to learn how to play golf. This aspect of golf is possibly even more important than helping to cultivate accountability for preparation. Accountability for preparation will eventually be the foundation of their future, no matter where God leads them.

Expecting children to go from video game, sugar-loving creatures to ball beating athletes over night is silly. Slowly implementing structure to their lives with habit calendars and simple drills while re-enforcing that preparation is the key to performance, however, is very possible. For the seven year old it may be three minutes or 25 reps with one drill. For the ten year old it may be six minutes or 50 reps with two drills. Again **responsibility and relevance go hand in hand.**

Also remember there is a big difference between random and block practice. Go back to the analogy in "Underwater BB Stacking." There are many research papers that show that block practice will lead to less retention of the skill. While random practice will be a more difficult and push your child, it will lead to higher retention. So when you see them zoned in for two minutes and then walk away don't start yelling at them. It is fine for them to break it up. One minute of intentional, deliberate, randomized practice is worth hours of "block" type practice with no purpose.

Much of this learning process relates to child development. I do not think age is as important as understanding your child or having the PGA Professional they work with understanding your child. The drills or exercises must be done each day, with the possibility of taking a couple of days off. The children should be held accountable for doing the drills and exercises. A time period or rep number that is too short is much better than one that is too long. These drills and exercises should be set up to fit nicely into the development and goals of your child. You should also be aware of the number of things the child is working on. For example, my seven year old is working on one thing. My nine year old is working on two things. Keep it simple. Keep it fun. Be very, very adamant about accomplishing their tasks each day and marking it off on their habit calendar.

Long before the college golfer you see working on their game each day with sweat rolling down their brow, something or someone taught them to be accountable. Whether it was a grandpa, a socio-economical situation, or simply a sport, they learned to be accountable in preparation for the desired outcome. They may have spent a little time at Disney World riding the rides, but they also cleaned up after themselves along the way!

Chapter Lessons:

- Disney World is a great place, but the aspects of Disney World should not be lived everyday by children that want to be great at a specific sport.
- Arm your children with the weapon of accountability
- Golf lessons work or don't work for a reason
- Expecting children to go from video game, sugar loving creatures to ball beating athletes overnight is an unrealistic expectation.
- Relevance and responsibility go hand in hand
- Trophies may be handed over at beautiful places but they are not earned there

Epilogue

Recently, a close friend and I had an in-depth conversation concerning the "business" side of golf instruction. We went back and forth with scenarios and solutions for nearly an hour. At one point I asked him, "Is your business really this complicated? Do you really have to learn all these different approaches to getting your employees to perform?" Without batting an eye his answer was, "Yes."

The ability to learn is necessary for success. After all, aren't we all driven? The ability to learn, however, does not just drop from a cloud. All of our "Eureka" moments come after hours of intense problem solving. The generation of children that will tote your last name around will need to learn these same lessons. That is, they will need to learn how to learn.

The environment they learn in is very much up to you, the parent. Golf is a vehicle for learning. For that matter, nearly every sport is a vehicle for learning. **Keep in mind that your children can learn from their performance or they can learn from the process.** Your child can learn that they are accountable for the performance (outcome) and adjust their preparation (process) after they are emotionally sabotaged. Preferably, your child can be held accountable for their preparation (process) and see the competition (outcome) as a means of demonstrating their preparation.

As you know, strategic planning starts with communicating with your child. Often, children and parents do not talk about goal setting until the children are in high school—which is woefully late. Think back for a moment about your own life. How many things have you wanted to be? Personally, I wanted to be a professional soccer player, a receiver for Joe Montana, a world champion boxer, and a Hall of Fame professional golfer. Did I accomplish any of these things? Did you accomplish all of your goals? But think of how empty we would be if we never had any goals.

Discuss "Goals."

The great thing about discussing goals early and then building a process to obtaining these goals is that children slowly learn to deal with failure. Slowly, day by day, they will wrap their arms around the process and embrace it. They will slowly be taught to become a champion through the process of failure.

Here is my suggestion. Sit down with your child and ask them to define a "goal." Chances are you will hear something like "To try to win something." Or you might hear, "To try and be somebody." You may even hear "Score a touchdown!"

After this conversation, explain to your child the difference between an **Outcome Oriented Goal, a Performance Oriented Goal, and a Process Oriented Goal**. An outcome goal is winning or achieving something. It is defeating the competition. A performance goal focuses on improvement in performance. An example of such a goal is holing ten putts in a row or hitting three draws on command. Process goals focus on improving form, movement, and strategy. While outcome goals are usually completely extrinsic, process goals are completely intrinsic.

Here is an example of an outcome goal: To win the state amateur championship. Here is an example of a performance goal: To average 74 in tournaments. Finally, here is an example of a process goal: To spend five minutes each day working on ball position in front of a mirror. Note again that the player is not in total control of either an outcome goal or a performance goal. Players are, however, in complete control of a process goal.

The reason I suggest that you discuss different goals early on with your children is that most children (or people) don't understand the differences among these goals. They don't understand how these three goals are interrelated. They don't understand which goal should come first. They don't understand the process.

Often times, the parents do not understand the process well themselves. Both outcome goals and performance goals are what many will call "practice." The goal is, of course, balance. Balance between achieving the outcome, seeing the performance increase, and a commitment to the everyday process goals. Parents must be aware that the temptation is always there for the outcome goal to take over. When that happens, the performance goals become too important and players easily stray from the process.

A Survey.

Recently, a survey was sent out by a state-run golf organization to examine perceptions about practicing golf. The questions were aimed at parents. I wanted to know what parents consider "practice" and also how much their children "practiced." Furthermore, I wanted to know why the kids were interested in golf in the first place. I believe the results are very compelling.

The first question in the survey was: **How many sports are your children involved in throughout the year?** The majority answer was two sports, with 32.6%. With 23.9%, the second most common response was (to me) disappointing: *one* sport. The response of three sports was a close 3rd with 21.7%. After that, however, only 13.0% were involved in four sports and only 8.7% were involved in five or more sports.

So what do the responses to this question mean? It means the majority of junior golfers are involved in golf and only one other sport. This means, barring some really great physical education classes and some very active parents, the majority of children are not playing enough sports to get their necessary training in physical literacy.

The second question: **If your child showed a true interest in a sport, at what age will you allow them to specialize in this sport?** The majority answer, at 36.2%, was 12 years of age. Through my research, I have found that specializing in one sport before puberty is not wise. Such a high response rate is also evidence that the temptation of specialization is rearing its head early. Second, at 27.1%, was the age of 14. While this response is consistent with some parents thinking that 12 years of age is a bit too young, 14 is also young. In fact, 16 would be a much better age to begin to specialize. Sadly, however, in the survey only 6.3% of the respondents considered 16 to be the correct age to begin to specialize.

The notion of specialization is near and dear to my heart. Unknowingly, by specializing early, we create compensations and/or dysfunctions in the bodies of our children. These compensations and dysfunctions are clear and present threats to their later development. It is not only the development of their physical bodies that is affected. The development of their minds is also affected. A strong, athletic, and functional body always leads to a stronger self-image. Furthermore, the risk of "burn out" runs higher with children that specialize at a young age.

Clearly, parents and children understand that you can't do everything to a high level. There are choices that must be made. Choosing too narrowly at too young of an age, however, means the children are likely setting themselves up for the possibility of emotional and physical compensations. Remember, age 16 or so should be the "point break" for specialization. Keeping active at sports wherein the child does NOT excel does help with golf. Why? Preparing their best for each sport and understanding the movement of sports in general is building a base for enhancing their golf swings.

The third question: **Why does your child play golf?** The response: *Because the child showed an interest at a young age,* had a response rate of 58.3%. Next, with 25%, was the response: *Because they wanted to play colle-*

giate golf. Recall that in the INSIGHTS chapters, we saw that children showed an interest in golf basically because the parents showed an interest in golf. So perhaps we are seeing evidence consistent with the importance of parental influence when a child is young.

So what does this mean? It means the children are coming to the sport of golf because parents exposed them to the game. When showing children the game of golf at a young age is fantastic, I believe that it also carries a responsibility. Candidly, it is my fervent hope that parents are teaching their children to have a growth mindset concerning the game of golf.

The fourth question: **Practice Is...** These were the possible answers: A) Hitting balls on the range; B) Working with an instructor; C) Doing drills at home, or; D) Playing golf in the afternoons. *Hitting balls on the driving range* was the winner with a whopping 72.9% of the answers. The next most popular answer was *doing drills at home,* with 58.3%. Playing in the afternoons came in third at 52.1% and working with an instructor was fourth at 39.6%. (Note that, on this question, more than one answer could be chosen.)

If you have read this book from the beginning, you know how I feel about driving ranges by now. They are convenient, but often, not efficient. The golf course and the mirror are much better places to grow a golf swing. The most unexplainable answer is parents that believe working with an instructor counts as *practice.* As an instructor, I will tell you that when your child is working with his or her teacher they are learning, not practicing. The reason someone like me and other PGA Teaching Professionals exist is to teach, or coach, students. That is, we give them instructions on what to practice.

So what do the answers to question four mean? It means the children and parents know they need to practice and the most convenient place to practice, in their minds, is the driving range. It sounds great, but I ask: Is the practice deliberate? Does the practice session on the range have intention? Are the children truly working on their swings or are they getting emotionally hijacked with ball flight?

Here is a good way of looking at it. If players, including your children, are intently working on ball flight, they are *playing*. If they are intently working on their mechanics, they are *practicing*. My advice is to mix the two concepts with extreme caution.

The fifth question: **Practice is performed...** The possible answers for this question were: A) Daily for ten minutes; B) Three times a week for 30 minutes; C) Twice weekly for one hour, or; D) Once weekly for more than two hours. At 53.5%, the majority answered that their children are *practicing three* *times a week for 30 minutes. Twice weekly for one hour* was the second most popular answer, at 34.9% in the survey. *Ten minutes daily* was third, bringing in 25.6%. It appears that only 18.6% are practicing once weekly for two hours.

So what does this mean? It means that children are working on their golf games the same way were are taught to do cardio! In some ways, it is good they are limiting their time if they are on the driving range during a practice session. Why? Limiting time means that the practice session can be more deliberate and intentional. On the other hand, the daily practice rate being so low means their little bodies and minds are not getting consistent enough movements to maximize gains.

The sixth question: **More time should be spent by your child...** The possible answers for this question were: A) Playing golf; B) Hitting golf balls (full swing); C) Chipping, or D) Putting. At 38.3%, the leading answer was *playing*. I completely agree! The kids need to be playing golf. At 34%, hitting balls came in second. Here is where it gets a bit crazy. *Chipping* came in at 14.9% and *putting* 12.8%!

What do the results of this question reveal? We see that children are not spending nearly enough time chipping and putting the golf ball. Chipping and putting are well over half the strokes played on the golf course. Statistically, I am proud the kids are playing, but I would bet they would all be so much better if they just began to stay off the driving range all together.

The seventh question: **Most of golf instruction is geared toward...** A) Building mental skills; B) Building physical skills (muscles and movements), or; C) Building technical skills. The responses formed a stair step. Technical skills came in first, Physical skills came in second, and Mental skills came in last, with only 21.3%. I often say there can only be three reasons of great play or poor play: The Body, The Mind or The Mechanics.

The results of this question suggest, to me, that parents and children are out of balance because building technical skills over-rides building mental skills. Look back at some of the interviews in this book. As if it were yesterday, I remember hearing a well-known sport psychologist say: "There are a million kids with great swings. That is not the problem." I can even tell you where we were standing when he said it. If I didn't understand what he was saying at the time, I certainly do now. Mom, Dad, child player, and coach think they can build a great swing and the mind will just catch up. Sadly, this is a mistaken belief.

The last question: **What more or less defines your child's practice?** The possible answers were A) daily, specific, slow; B) often, defined, hitting balls; C) weekly, target oriented, playing, or; D) sporadically, random, no hitting balls. Close race here. Answer (A) was chosen 31.3% of the time, and Answer (B) was chosen 29.2% of the time. Weekly, target oriented, playing came in at 25%--a close third, while Answer (D) received 14.6% of the responses.

Do you remember the golf course manager in "HUH?" saying something to the effect of parents not being honest with their children (in terms of golf)? I think this can explain why over 60% of the parents truly *believe* the children are practicing daily, specifically, and in a defined way. Yet this allegedly deliberate practice occurs (according to the survey) only three days per week for 30 minutes.

Conversations.

Let's look at two imaginary conversations. The first one is my attempt to summarize how we could see such results to the survey. The second one is my attempt to summarize what I would like to see in an attempt to build the process underlying the behavior of champions.

First Conversation.

One day, a parent asks the child, "What are your goals in golf?"

The child responds, "I don't know. Maybe to get better and maybe win a tournament?"

"Ok, great," responds the parent. "Maybe you could aim at playing college golf?"

"If I can get good enough, sure," says the child.

"Well right now you are playing two sports. So by age 12 or 14 we, your parents, expect you to pick one sport if that is ok," says the parent.

"Okay," says the child.

The parent begins to talk about setting up a plan. "Now in order for you to accomplish your goals, we need to set up a plan. In order for you to get better at golf, and maybe win a tournament, where do you think you need to spend most of your time?" asks the parent.

"Hitting balls on the range!" says the child.

"Absolutely," agrees the parent. I can't think of a better place for you practice and get closer to your goal of getting better and winning a tournament! Now how much time do you think we will need to get the job done?" asks the parent.

"Maybe 3 times a week for 30 minutes?" Answers the child (because he sees his parents exercise on such a schedule).

"That sounds great. But what are you going to be working on?" asks the parent.

"Playing," says the child.

"Well you can't play at the driving range can you?" asks the parent.

"I mean hitting balls!" says the child.

"There you go! You are going to be hitting balls. We will go play some on the weekends," says the parent.

"Wow, fun! Should I chip and putt?" asks the child.

"I don't really think so. Why don't you just concentrate on hitting balls and building a good swing...I have surprise for you if you will do your practice too!"

"What is that?"

"I am going to get you lessons so that your technical skills of swinging the club get better and better. You are going to build yourself a great golf swing I bet! Are you excited?" asks the parent.

"I sure am. Thanks!" says the child.

This sample conversation, to me, summarizes the responses from the survey. Does this conversation really sound like the way for this child to accomplish their goal? Note that this conversation has produced an outcome goal. There are no performance goals. Just a few performance goals go a long way. The process goal is to go to the range three days each week. At the range, however, what will be emphasized? From the conversation, we really do not know.

Second Conversation.

"Hey let's talk about golf. What might be one of your goals?" asks the parent.

"To get better, I guess. If I get could get better, I would like to win a tournament!" says the child.

The parent asks, "What kind of tournament? A state sanctioned tournament, a local tournament, a club tournament?"

"I don't really know. I guess maybe a local tournament, and then maybe a sanctioned tournament," says the child

"Okay. Well let's make winning a local tournament your big goal. We will change it to a state tournament when you accomplish the first goal. Now what scores will you need to shoot to win a local tournament?" asks the parent.

"38 or 40, I think," says the child.

"I agree. So why don't we put shooting 38 as one of your performance goals. We will take you to Baskin Robbins when you accomplish it!" says the parent. "In fact we will set 46, 44, 42, and 40 as performance goals. Each time you accomplish scoring a new low, we can all go to Baskin Robbins!"

"Awesome!" replies the child.

"Now what do you think some of the things you are going to need to work on to accomplish your performance goals?" asks the parent.

"My swing. Hitting the ball straight and a little longer. My score...." says the child.

"Yes that is right. You are going to need to improve everything. Your mind a little, your technique a little, your short game a little, your strategy a little. You get it huh?" asks the parent.

"Kinda," responds the child.

"Well now we need some goals called process goals. These goals are not quite as fun, but they sure are important. These goals are things that you must do every day. When you do them every day, you are accomplishing your performance goals. Now I know you are not a huge fan of having to run with the track team, but that running is really helping your body get stronger. I also know you are not a big fan of gymnastics or karate. But, both of these activities are making you stronger too. When you do these other sports, you will be building a strong and athletic body to bring to the golf course. You will need to work around all these activities, so let's plan this out," says the parent.

"So that is why you make me go to that stupid gym? I always wondered why," says the child.

The parent chuckles, "That is right! Now you will have three days each week for the next two months to work on your golf game. Let's break it up," says the parent. "First you need to play. Just improve your strategy of playing golf and getting the ball around the course. It is not so important what you score. When you go out to play, I want you to concentrate on what you are thinking. Don't worry about where the ball goes. After it goes where it goes, it is where it is. You can't go back and change it. So, find the ball, and figure out what to do next. When you do that, you are working on strategy and thinking," says the parent.

"Should I be thinking about a bad shot or good shot?" asks the child.

"Well, we must look at where we are. Focus on the present and focus on your next shot. It's hard to do, but don't worry about where the ball goes. You have to learn to focus on things that you can control. The one thing you can control is yourself."

"Oh, that's why my older brother got in trouble for not cleaning up his room, but I did clean up my room and I did not get into trouble!" says the child.

"Correct! So why don't we make it a goal for you to go out one afternoon each week and just play a few holes. Play as many or few as you want really, but you must do it concentrating on you are thinking and not where the ball goes. Alright?" asks the parent.

"Ok. I could play 16, then 13, 14, and 15 if the weather wasn't looking good. Or, I could play 16, 17, 18, 1, 2, and 3! Or, I could start on four and play all nine holes right back to three!" says the child.

"Right! You got it! Now, what is also really important to scoring?" asks the parent.

"Hitting the ball!" exclaims the child.

"Yes it is. But chipping and putting are really your best weapons. Just look at Tiger Woods or Luke Donald or Lee Westwood. Sure they hit the ball great, but they really carve off the shots with the short game. So one day per week, you will practice chipping and putting ok?" asks the parent.

"Yeah. I remember that putt Tiger made at the US Open on the last hole. That was cool," says the child.

"To accomplish your goals of winning a local tournament and one of your performance goal of shooting 38 how much time do you think you need to spend chipping and putting?" asks the parent.

"Maybe an hour?" asks the child.

"That sounds reasonable, but only if you are getting something out of that hour," says the parent.

"And not just banging balls around the green like my friend Leon does," says the child.

"Exactly. Have you ever watched Mr. Tim practice? He practices getting the ball up and down. He will take one ball, his putter, and a wedge to the green and practice hitting the chip and making the putt. Do you think that is something you could do?" asks the parent.

"For an hour. One day a week. Yes," says the child.

"Great. Well your second process goal is to practice chipping and putting with one ball one hour each week. Now how about your full swing? What do you think you need to work on?"

"Well the last lesson Mr. Wilkes gave me was on ball position. He wanted me to put some sticks down on the ground," says the child.

"Great. Well why don't you practice your ball position for one hour on the range on your third day? Instead of hitting the same club why don't you go through your whole bag and aim at different target? Maybe you could hit four shots with every club or something like that," says the parent.

"I can do that," says the child.

"But the sticks must be laid down right?" asks the parent.

"Right. Because if they are not I may get confused and start doing something else," says the child.

"Great. We have a plan," says the parent. "Each week you are going to work on your ball position for an hour. Second, each week you are going to chip and putt with one ball for one hour. Third, you are going to go out and play focusing on yourself one day each week. Does that sound like a good plan for you to accomplish your goal of winning a local tournament, and a good way to earn some ice cream by accomplishing your performance goals?"

"Yes sir," answers the child.

"Well we are going to tape these weekly goals to the refrigerator. Each week, it is your responsibility to accomplish these goals. After a month of doing them, I will make sure we get you a lesson and you are heading in the right direction. OK?" asks the parent.

"Alright!" exclaims the child.

Now which child has a better chance? Go back to Hendrix's lyrics. "Many moons passed and the dream grew strong until tomorrow he would sing his first war song and fight his first battle but something went wrong…" Go back to the above examples. Go back to the data the survey reported. Go back and think about when things began to go wrong or right. Go back and think about how the plan changed or altered course a bit. Go back and figure out how that fun loving kid that was interested in golf is now losing his passion. Go back and figure out how that fun loving kid is now on the PGA Tour. Go back and figure out what the game has taught you.

I caution you not to play any blame games here. Everything in this book is reversible. Everything in this book can be layered a little deeper also. It is not "your" fault or "the instructor's" fault. Just tweak your process a bit. Put some rules in that you, your children, and your family, can be held accountable for accomplishing.

In closing I would to suggest this: Put your time where your heart is. Know **Who** is in control of your heart before you put your time there. Once the time is being put there, grade your success carefully.

Oh yeah….. make sure you listen to great music too! Especially Dexter Gordon and Pearl Jam.

Old Waverly's Junior Golf Camp

If you are looking for top-level technical, mental, and physical instruction at one of America's greatest golf venues you are at the right place.

The world today of junior sports is different today in many respects. Organized sports have put an emphasis on "winning." While winning is an outcome we all strive for, the process of preparation is the key to unlocking potential.

"To promote a growth mind-set among young adults using the game of golf."

The road to being average is much easier than that of being a competitor. Many young adults can get lost in this process. They can begin to think that frustration, set backs, and difficulties along the way are items that other competitors have not faced. The reality is the road to becoming a champion has many hills and valleys. Setting outcome or performance goals without process goals is simply incomplete and can lead to immense frustration.

"To give junior golfers the tools of success in a fun, disciplined, defined, and caring southern golf culture."

With the correct "tools" junior golfers can understand their outcome or performance is tied to the process of preparation they use everyday. To change the outcome they must first change the process. Here juniors learn the process is really quite simple but has many facets.

Here you will find an approach that is a mixture of mechanical, physical, and mental fundamentals. Getting better at golf is not all about hitting great shots or having great swings. Here a mixture of learning the short game, putting, and the full swing is taught and learned. Getting better at golf isn't all about winning. Here junior golfers will come to understand the things they are in control of such as their strategy, their routines, and their preparation.

When the kids are here they can expect a lot of on and off course instruction. Time is spent teaching the juniors not only what to practice but how to practice. Time is spent teaching the juniors not only how to hit a particular shot but also when to use it on the course. Time is spent teaching the juniors not only how to succeed but also the behaviors that will lead to the successful mind set on and off the course.

"Foremost to promote strong minds and prepare junior golfers for the enjoyment of competitive golf and life."

www.oldwaverly.com
vj@troliogolf.com

Bibliography

Canadian Sport For Life (CS4L)

Bassham, Lanny. *With Winning In Mind.* The United States of America:1995.

Burke, Jr. Jackie, *It's Only A Game,* New York, New York: Penguin Group, 2006

Colvin, Geoff. *Talent is Overrated.* New York.: Penguin Group, 2008.

Covey, Stephen R., *The 7 Habits of Highly Effective People,* New York, NY: Simon and Schuster, 1989.

Coyle, Daniel. *The Talent Code.* New York, New York: Bantam Dell, 2009.

Dweck, Carol S. *Mindset: The New Psychology of Success.* New York: Ballantine Books, 2006.

Egoscue, Pete. *Pain Free.* Bantam Books: 1998.

Egoscue, Pete. *The Egoscue Method of Health Through Motion.* New York: HarperCollins Publishers, 1992.

Fancher, Bob, Ph.D. *The Pleasure of Small Motions.* Guildford, CT: Lyons Press, 2000.

Gladwell, Malcolm. *Blink.* New York, New York: Little Bay Books/Little, Brown and Company. 2005

Godin, Seth. *The Dip.* New York, New York: Penguin Group, 2007.

Greenburg, Dan. *How To Make Yourself Miserable.* New York: Random House, 1966.

Keeler, O.B, *The Bobby Jones Story*, Chicago, Illinois: Triumph Book, 2003.

Murphy, Michael, *Golf In The Kingdom,* New York, New York: Penguin Group, 1972

Rotella, Dr. Bob, *The Golfer's Mind*, New York, NY: Simon & Schuster, 2004.

Sampson, Curt, *Hogan,* Nashville, TN: Rutledge Hill Press,1996.

Syed, Mathew. *BOUNCE.* New York: HarperCollins Publishers, 2010.

Titleist Performance Institute, TPI Level 1, JC 2 & 3: Achusnet Compay.

Weiner, David. *Battling The Inner Dummy.* Amherst, New York: Prometheus Books, 1999.